翻转人生的
15堂英语课

吴宜铮 ◎ 著

北京理工大学出版社
BEIJING INSTITUTE OF TECHNOLOGY PRESS

How to Use
使用这本书的方式

使用这本书的诀窍

1. 别急着埋头背单词,先想办法理解内容。
2. 根据兴趣,从不同的主题开始学习。
3. 以对话或文章为基础,延伸学习句型与单词。
4. 一次学好听力、口说、阅读、写作。
5. 随时聆听 MP3,同步加强英语听说能力。

如何将英语能力由负转正?

停止抱怨,认真学习。停止无意义的背诵学习,用灵活的方式,学到够用一辈子的英语,用高中程度的英语,培养一辈子受用的英语能力。

很多学习者拿到一本英语学习书时,不管这本书的主题是单词、会话还是语法,常常一翻开就不分青红皂白地开始埋头背记。这种"死读书"的方式,已不再适用于现在这个变化万千的社会了!

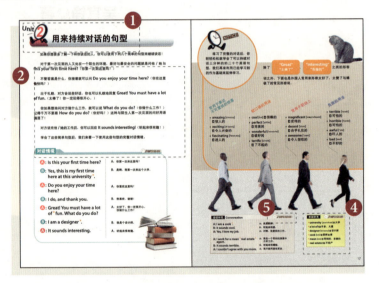

1 主题涵盖"发音、人际、运动、电影、食物、旅行、购物、工作"

从基础发音开始,扩展人际关系,和他人讨论运动、电影、美食,去国外旅行、购物,并和外国人一起工作!

2 清楚中文讲解,搭配实用英语范例

在英语能力不够好的情况下,全英语的教材反而会让学习者感到更加恐惧。透过清楚的中文解说,并搭配实用的英语范例,可让读者一次就搞懂学习内容。

3 举一反三的万用句型

根据对话情境、短文范例,归纳整理出超级实用的英语句型,并在范例中以编号标示,方便读者查找学习。

4 别让补充单词成为学习的阻碍

在阅读中,难免会看到一些不是很了解的单词,停下来查找太浪费时间,也会打乱学习步骤,在阅读时先跳过,理解全文的意思即可,在每个单元的最后,可将不可不知的补充单词整理出来!

5 MP3 随身听,听说能力随时练

由两位(一男一女)美籍专业录音员录制对话、精选会话、单词等英语内容,读者可下载MP3,戴上耳机、拿着手机,随时听、随时读、随时学。

6 不会太难、一定要会的语法教室

根据学习主题,补充一定要会的英语语法。别听到语法就害怕!本书的语法难度约符合高中程度,只要学会最基础简单的语法,就有机会翻转你的英语能力!

7 实境照片、模拟视窗,让学习内容和现实生活更加紧密结合

如果你一直有"书是书、生活是生活"这样的想法,背再多英语也没有用,本书通过清楚又活泼的排版方式,搭配实境照片,并模拟信息出现的视窗,让书跟生活更加紧密结合。

学习内容地图检索
15天的学习内容、翻转人生的15堂英语课与学习重点,一目了然。→请见 P.004

能力测验量表
3个问题、3个答案,看看你的英语能力到了哪种程度。→请见 P.008

QRcode 下载音频
想要带着手机,随时听英语对话,走到哪、学到哪,就一定要从这里下载音频。

翻转人生的 15堂英语课

用15堂英语课,提升你的英语能力!
有兴趣的东西,最能够引起学习动力,本书用最贴近生活的15堂英语课,帮你提升你的英语能力!

用30分钟的学习,逆转你的人生!
30分钟的通勤时间,你可以穿行半个城市;30分钟的用餐时间,你可以吃完一份麦当劳套餐;每天30分钟的学习时间,你可以逆转自己的人生!

英语能力由负转正,人生就此逆转胜!
英语是全球通用的语言,但不是你碰到的每个外国人都来自英语系国家,只要学会这15堂课,只要勇敢开口说英语,你的人生就能逆转胜!

Contents & Learning Map
目录 & 学习地图

What kind of service do you want today?

Day 1

发音篇

Lesson 1
想学好英语，从发音开始！ ▶ P. 01

- 学习重点 1　见词就能发音
- 学习重点 2　掌握短元音、长元音、双元音
- 学习重点 3　从单词、短句到短文，都能轻松开口说

Day 2-3

人际篇

Lesson 2
一起用英语交朋友！ ▶ P. 13

- 学习重点 1　用简单的英语和外国人寒暄
- 学习重点 2　用简单的句型，扩展与延伸对话
- 学习重点 3　和朋友在社群媒体上用英语聊天
- 学习重点 4　运用基本的 5W1H 句型，进行自我介绍
- 学习重点 5　活用不同句型与排列组合，让自我介绍更加丰富

Lesson 3
在办公室会用到的英语！ ▶ P. 27

- 学习重点 1　写 E-mail 向客户询价
- 学习重点 2　学会电话英语的 SOP 流程
- 学习重点 3　掌握从机场接机到公司接待的英语会话
- 学习重点 4　写封英语贺卡，延续双方的互动

Where do you see yourself in five years?

Day 4-5
运动篇

Lesson 4
席卷全球的运动热潮！　▶ P. 39

- 学习重点 1　通过体育新闻，仿写文章
- 学习重点 2　看懂短篇体育新闻
- 学习重点 3　和人讨论喜欢的球队与球星
- 学习重点 4　简短介绍喜欢的运动

Lesson 5
世界瞩目的运动赛事！　▶ P. 51

- 学习重点 1　讨论奥运比赛
- 学习重点 2　看懂足球比赛的报道
- 学习重点 3　了解并阐述比赛的历史来源

Major League Baseball!!

Day 6-7
电影篇

Lesson 6
不可不知的电影二三事！　▶ P. 61

- 学习重点 1　约外国朋友看电影
- 学习重点 2　用英语和朋友讨论喜欢的电影
- 学习重点 3　通过电影内容，了解国际通用的分级制度
- 学习重点 4　列举并用英语介绍经典名片

Lesson 7
那些电影教我的英语！　▶ P. 71

- 学习重点 1　用英语邀请别人看电影
- 学习重点 2　买票、买爆米花、看电影
- 学习重点 3　观看国外的电影颁奖典礼实况转播
- 学习重点 4　熟悉并引用经典电影台词

Don't move. Give me the suitcase.

Contents & Learning Map
目录 & 学习地图

Day 8-9
食物篇

Lesson 8
大快朵颐的时间到了！ ▶ P. 81

- 学习重点 1　掌握用英语点餐的三步骤
- 学习重点 2　认识吃进肚子的食物
- 学习重点 3　看懂相关报刊文章
- 学习重点 4　阅读并理解文章的理念

Lesson 9
一起采买食材，下厨吧！ ▶ P. 91

- 学习重点 1　准备采购前，不可不知的会话
- 学习重点 2　找篇食谱，洗手做羹汤
- 学习重点 3　知道异国美食的英语说法
- 学习重点 4　和食物相关的英语惯用语

Day 10-11
旅行篇

Lesson 10
去国外开开眼界吧！ ▶ P. 101

- 学习重点 1　找到想享受的国外旅游行程
- 学习重点 2　看懂国外观光景点的相关资料
- 学习重点 3　在国外网站上订机票
- 学习重点 4　预订想住的饭店

> I can't believe it. What a noble view!

Lesson 11
收拾行李，出发旅行去！ ▶ P. 111

- 学习重点 1　准备去国外旅行
- 学习重点 2　到国外的机场报到登机
- 学习重点 3　用英语和饭店人员沟通

Day 12-13

购物篇

Lesson 12
趁着购物季，大肆采买吧！ ▶ P. 125

- 学习重点 1　到国外的实体店大采购
- 学习重点 2　和外国店员进行对话
- 学习重点 3　用英语询价与议价

Lesson 13
网络购物超方便！ ▶ P. 135

- 学习重点 1　在国外网站上购物
- 学习重点 2　用英语询问订购内容
- 学习重点 3　和购物有关的英语用语

Day 14-15

工作篇

Lesson 14
一定要知道的职场英语！ ▶ P. 147

- 学习重点 1　撰写英语求职信
- 学习重点 2　进行英语面试
- 学习重点 3　用英语向公司做自我介绍

Lesson 15
用英语在职场发光发热！ ▶ P. 159

- 学习重点 1　用英语进行晨会汇报
- 学习重点 2　撰写英语电子邮件
- 学习重点 3　用英语和客户开会
- 学习重点 4　和国外同事闲聊
- 学习重点 5　到外商公司参访
- 学习重点 6　进行员工教育训练

You'd better arrive there in 30 minutes or our manager will be very angry.

07

Simple Test
你的英文能力达到哪种程度呢?

Question 1

想要在网络上购物,但有些国外网站偏偏没有中文版,网络代购又有诈骗的风险,面对网络上琳琅满目的产品,你知道怎么把它们买回家吗?

Question 2

去一家公司面试的时候,临时被面试官要求做1分钟左右的英语自我介绍,叙述内容包括姓名、兴趣、家庭状况、座右铭,你知道要怎么开口说吗?

Question 3

中文会话中最常出现的"因为……所以……"的句型,每个单词你都认得,但你知道英语的正确说法吗?

Answer

善用 5 个 WH、1 个 How 的问句进行自我介绍，让自我介绍不再只是简单的 "Hello, my name is _____. I am from China."。

［句型］

❶ Who am I? 我是谁？
❷ What do I do? 我做什么？
❸ Where do I come from? 我来自哪里？
❹ What is my motto? 我的格言是什么？
❺ Why do I believe in my motto?
 我为什么相信我的格言？
❻ How do I feel about myself? 我怎样看自己？

恭喜你，已经通过 Lesson 2 的课程了！

Lesson 2

Answer

购物网站的功能就是，搜寻、新增至购物车、结账、断续购物、联络资料、送出订单……只要看得懂这些英语，你的购物足迹就能遍及全世界。

search engine 搜寻引擎
add to Shopping Cart 新增至购物车
checkout 结账
continue shopping 继续购物
contact and delivery details 联络与送货详细资料
submit 送出
proceed 处理
order confirmation 订货确认单

恭喜你，已经通过 Lesson 13 的课程了！

Lesson 13

Answer

because（因为）、so（所以）、although（虽然）、but（但是）这些连接词，因为属性不同，在同一个句子中不能一起出现！请记得下列句型

Because of + 名词，主语 + 动词
Because + 主语 + 动词（附属从句），主语 + 动词（主要从句）
主语 + 动词 because of + 名词
主语 + 动词（主要从句）because + 主语 + 动词（附属从句）

恭喜你，已经通过 Lesson 6 的课程了！

Lesson 6

Lesson 1
想学好英语,从发音开始!

学习重点 1 | 见词就能发音
学习重点 2 | 掌握短元音、长元音、双元音
学习重点 3 | 从单词、短句到短文,都能轻松开口说

见词发音的辅音

发音（pronunciation）是什么呢？很多人学不好英语，其实问题是从发音开始的。为什么？因为英语字母只有 26 个，发音却不只 26 个。

举例来说，单词 bat（蝙蝠、球棒）有三个字母，它刚好就有三个音，念法为 [bæt]，但是 batch（批次），这个词有五个字母，它的发音却是 [bætʃ]，只有三个音。怎么会这样呢？因为英语的发音不只是 26 个字母的单独发音，它包括了元音和辅音。

在发音中，辅音比较简单，大多是见词发音，什么叫作见词发音？
bat（蝙蝠）、batch（批次）中的 b、t、th 就分别念成 [b]、[t] 和 [tʃ]。那要如何知道是字母还是音标？音标会用括号 [ ] 来标示，所以 b 是字母，[b] 是音标。这个道理就像是我们看到了车子，但是听到的声音是车子的啸鸣声一样，有形体，也有声响。

而元音又分成短元音、长元音、双元音和半元音；辅音则有清辅音与浊辅音。英语字母的发音有许多规则，但是例外的也很多。我们来看看如何化繁为简地学习英语发音。

有趣的统计数字！

英语有 26 个字母，a、e、i、o、u 是元音字母，其他 21 个是辅音字母。
英语音标包括元音与辅音，共 41 个，元音 17 个，辅音 24 个。

见词发音的辅音

♪ MP3 01-01

字母	音标	字母	音标	字母	音标
b	[b]	k	[k]	s	[s]
c	[k]	l	[l]	t	[t]
d	[d]	m	[m]	v	[v]
f	[f]	n	[n]	w	[w]
g	[g]	p	[p]	x	[ks]
h	[h]	q	[kw]	y	[j]
j	[dʒ]	r	[r]	z	[z]

Lesson 1

在这 21 个辅音字母当中，可再分成清辅音与浊辅音。差别就在于发音时手指头摸着喉咙，念出清辅音时，没有振动，而念出浊辅音时，则会振动。

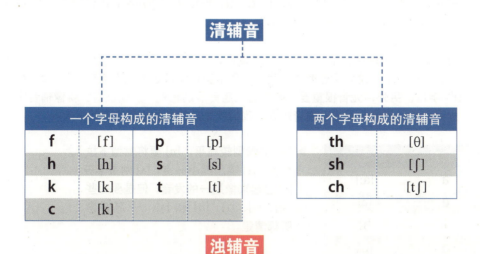

一个字母构成的清辅音				两个字母构成的清辅音	
f	[f]	p	[p]	th	[θ]
h	[h]	s	[s]	sh	[ʃ]
k	[k]	t	[t]	ch	[tʃ]
c	[k]				

见字母发声的浊辅音				一个以上的字母组成的浊辅音	
b	[b]	r	[r]	th	[ð]、[θ]
d	[d]	v	[v]	g、s、su、si	[ʒ]
g	[g]	w	[w]	j、g	[dʒ]
l	[l]	y	[j]	ng、nk	[ŋ]
m	[m]	z	[z]		
n	[n]				

- 字母 l 的发音也比较特别，在元音前，与元音拼音，发音类似"勒"，是浊辅音；与元音拼音或在词尾时，发音类似"欧"。
- 另外，y 如果在词首会发 [j] 的音，在词尾则发 [ɪ] 或 [aɪ] 的音。
- 辅音字母就像我们学习 26 个英语字母一样要常练习！尤其要注意，辅音为无声或有声，[b] 和 [p]、[k] 和 [g]、[v] 和 [f] 一定要搞清楚。

Unit 2 短元音 a、e、i、o、u

幼儿园小朋友都会说的 "a、e、i、o、u, baby, I love you." 道出了英语发音中最重要的元音字母 "a、e、i、o、u"。

为什么元音字母这么重要？因为在英语中，元音决定了发音中的音节。每个英语词都至少有一个音节，这句话也就告诉我们，每个英语词都必须至少含有一个 "a、e、i、o、u" 字母；另外，元音很重要，因为它决定音节的轻重，影响发音。就像辅音字母有发音规则一样，元音字母也有发音规则，我们就先从简单的短元音开始学起。

短元音 a、e、i、o、u	
a	[æ]
e	[ɛ]
i	[ɪ]
o	[ɑ]
u	[ʌ]

▶ [æ] 的嘴型较扁平，[ɑ] 要将嘴型下拉、全开，[ɛ] 嘴型缩小一点，[ʌ] 则是半开，[ɪ] 念起来像是一的发音，但是要短些。[æ]、[ɛ]、[ɪ]、[ɑ] 和 [ʌ]，一定要念、听都清楚。

学会了这五个短元音的发音后，我们要进行拼音练习！先进行 a、e、i、o、u 放在词首的发音练习。利用之前介绍过的见词发音辅音加上短元音，就可以顺利地读出单词。

首先，先进行 a、e、i、o、u 放在词首的发音练习　　♪ MP3 01-02

a [æ]		
at [æt]	p	在……
ax [æks]	n	斧头
act [ækt]	n 法案	v 行动
ant [ænt]	n	蚂蚁
and [ænd]	c	和

e [ɛ]		
egg [ɛg]	n	蛋
edit [ˈɛdɪt]	v	编辑
end [ɛnd]	n / v	结束
envy [ˈɛnvɪ]	v	忌妒、羡慕
empty [ˈɛmptɪ]	a	空的

i [ɪ]

if [ɪf]	c 如果
is [ɪz]	v 是（第三人称 be 动词）
ill [ɪl]	a 生病的
inch [ɪntʃ]	n 英寸
itchy [ˈɪtʃɪ]	a 痒的

o [a]

on [an]	p 在……上面
odd [ad]	a 奇数的、奇怪的
opt [apt]	v 选择
ox [aks]	n 牛
object [ˈabdʒɪkt]	n 物品

u [ʌ]

up [ʌp]	ad 向上
ugly [ˈʌglɪ]	a 难看的
uncle [ˈʌŋkl]	n 叔伯
us [ʌs]	pr 我们
upset [ʌpˈsɛt]	v 扰乱

注意 由两个音节（元音）构成的词得念出重音，像 upset [ʌpˈsɛt] v 干扰，重音就放在第二个上。

接下来，进一步练习 a、e、i、o、u 放在辅音字母之间的发音 ♪ MP3 01-03

a [æ]

bat [bæt]	n 蝙蝠
fat [fæt]	n 脂肪
hat [hæt]	n 帽子
lamp [læmp]	n 灯
snap [snæp]	v 折断 n 噼啪声

e [ɛ]

bet [bɛt]	v 打赌
leg [lɛg]	n 腿
bench [bɛntʃ]	n 长椅
get [gɛt]	v 获得
yet [jɛt]	c 然而

i [ɪ]	
live [lɪv]	v 生活
chip [tʃɪp]	n 芯片、碎片、筹码
ship [ʃɪp]	n 船只
visit ['vɪzɪt]	n/v 拜访
will [wɪl]	n 意志 v 将

o [a]	
dot [dat]	n 点
frog [frag]	n 青蛙
dodge [dadʒ]	v 闪避
not [nat]	v 不是
box [baks]	n 盒子

u [ʌ]	
lunch [lʌntʃ]	n 午餐
bunch [bʌntʃ]	n 束
bug [bʌg]	n 虫
hug [hʌg]	n 拥抱
mug [mʌg]	n 马克杯

使用单词记忆卡：闪卡

闪卡就是把单词写在卡片上，透过卡片来刺激视觉与辨识力。它可以让你的英语学习更有趣，也可以检查你的元音学习是否正确扎实。英语的学习就像储蓄与练功一样，要每天坚持，培养实力，为了避免死记硬背的无趣，可以使用各种新方法来改善学习与增加乐趣。

检查一下，看看你的短元音跟辅音学得如何，把下列的单词、短语、句子和文章大声读出来！ ♪ MP3 01-04

- a **bug**（虫）
- on a **mug**（马克杯）
- a **big hug**（一个大拥抱）
- A **bug** on a **mug** with a **big hug** impressed us.
  上面有一个大拥抱虫图案的马克杯令我们印象深刻。

This is Uncle Sam. Uncle Sam has ten cats, not ten cups. Yes, Uncle Sam has ten cats. His ten cats like fish not apples. His pretty cats in red socks amaze us. Upon his desk, Uncle Sam has ten amazing cats in red socks. Uncle Sam lives with his ten cats, and he thinks this simple pleasure with ten cats is fun.

这是山姆大叔。山姆大叔有十只猫，不是十个杯子。是的，山姆大叔有十只猫。他的十只猫喜欢鱼，不喜欢苹果。那穿着红袜子的漂亮猫咪让我们觉得很惊奇。在他的书桌上，有十只穿着红袜子的有趣猫咪。山姆大叔和他的十只猫咪一起生活，他认为与十只猫的简单生活很有趣。

Unit 3 短元音 [ɔ]、[ɚ]、[ɜ]、[ʊ] 加上弱元音 [ə]

除了上述的短元音外，还有短元音 [ɔ]、[ɚ]、[ɜ]、[ʊ]，我们来看看哪些字母常发这些音，每个音我们都会练习五个词。

♪ MP3 01-05

[ɔ]
- walk [wɔk]　　　v 走路
- pause [pɔz]　　　v 暂停
- boss [bɔs]　　　n 老板
- draw [drɔ]　　　v 画图
- strawberry [ˈstrɔbɛrɪ]　n 草莓

★ al、au、aw、o 的 [ɔ]，嘴巴要张大。

[ɜ]
- bird [bɜd]　　　n 鸟
- burst [bɜst]　　　v 爆裂
- work [wɜk]　　　n/v 工作
- earth [ɜθ]　　　n 地球
- nurse [nɜs]　　　n 护士

★ ir、ur、or、er 的 [ɜ]，重音节卷舌。

[ɚ]
- after [ˈæftɚ]　　　ad 在……之后
- familiar [fəˈmɪljɚ]　a 熟悉的
- author [ˈɔθɚ]　　　n 作者
- sister [ˈsɪstɚ]　　　n 姐妹
- beggar [ˈbɛgɚ]　　n 乞丐

★ er、ar、or 的 [ɚ]，轻音节卷舌。

[ʊ]
- book [bʊk]　　　n 书
- cook [kʊk]　　　n 厨师
- wood [wʊd]　　　n 木头
- put [pʊt]　　　v 放置
- good [gʊd]　　　a 好的

★ u、oo 常发 [ʊ]，发音时要嘟嘴巴。

[ə]
- afraid [əˈfred]　　v 害怕的
- system [ˈsɪstəm]　　n 系统
- animal [ˈænəml]　　n 动物
- abandon [əˈbændən]　v 放弃
- cheerful [ˈtʃɪrfəl]　ad 欢乐的

★ 不在重音节上的 a、e、i、o、u 发 [ə]。

07

接下来要练习单词、句子和文章，大声念出来喔！ ♪ MP3 01-06

- **elephants** 大象
  ↓
- About **Elephants**. 关于大象。
  ↓
- **Elephant** is the God of luck. 大象是好运之神。
  ↓
- **Elephants** bring good luck. 大象带来好运。
  ↓
- How can **elephants** help us to earn the good luck?
  大象如何让我们赢得好运？
  ↓
- To put trunks of **elephants** upwards represents the arrival of good luck.
  把象牙朝上放置代表着好运降临。

There are many famous churches in the world. Some are small, and others are big. There are even old and modern churches. Churches are not simple. They are wonderful and rich in historical colors. Constructing churches often takes more than ten years.

- church [tʃɜtʃ] n 教堂
- cathedral [kə'θidrəl] n 大教堂
- ode [od] n 颂歌
- psalm [sɑm] n 赞美诗
- ambo ['æmbo] n 读经台
- the Bible [ðə 'baɪbl] n 圣经
- priest [prist] n 神父

世界上有许多知名的教堂。有些教堂小，有些教堂很大。甚至有些教堂历史悠久但看似现代。教堂建筑不简单。它们有卓越且丰富的历史色彩。建造教堂通常需要十年以上的时间。

Unit 4 不是只将音节拉长的长元音 [i]、[e]、[o]、[u]

为什么要特别强调长元音不是只把音节拉长？因为和 [ɪ]、[ɛ]、[a]、[ʌ]、[u] 等短元音比起来，长元音 [i]、[e]、[o]、[u] 发音时不仅必须将尾音拉长，你的舌头也要放对位置。例如，发 [i] 的舌头位置比发 [ɪ] 来得高，舌头也可感觉到比较多的压力。我们马上来学习这些发音。

♪ MP3 01-07

e_e、ee、ea、ey 常发 [i]

ease [iz]	n	安逸 v 放松
see [si]	v	看见
teach [titʃ]	v	教导
leaf [lif]	n	叶子
key [ki]	n	钥匙

a_e、ai、ay 常发 [e]

ace [es]	n	王牌
wake [wek]	v	苏醒
fail [fel]	v	失败
tail [tel]	n	尾巴
bay [be]	n	海湾

o_e、oe、oa、ow 常发 [o]

poke [pok]	v	戳
smoke [smok]	n	烟雾 v 抽烟
toast [tost]	n	吐司
toe [to]	n	脚趾
low [lo]	a	低的

u_e、ue、ew、ui 常发 [u]

pure [pjur]	a	纯洁的
nude [njud]	a	赤裸的
sue [su]	v	控告
hew [hju]	v	砍、劈
bruise [bruz]	n	瘀青

学习最后的双元音之前，我们还得把下列的词语、句子和文章大声念出来。 ♪ MP3 01-08

- **Faces** 面貌

  ↓

- **Faces** of Mother Nature.
  大自然的各种面貌。

  ↓

- **Faces** of Mother Nature at Different Places.
  在不同地方大自然的各种面貌。

  ↓

- **Faces** of mother nature at different places take your breath away.
  在不同地方大自然的各种面貌令你屏息。

  ↓

- Our planes take you to see **faces** of mother nature at different places that take your breath away.
  我们的飞机带你到不同地方去见识令你屏息的大自然的各种面貌。

  ↓

- Our planes take you to see **faces** of mother nature at different places that take your breath away, and those experiences teach you to cope with changes in your life.
  我们的飞机带你到不同地方去见识令你屏息的大自然的各种面貌，而这些经验可以教导你应对生命中的改变。

A <u>cave</u> is <u>known</u> as a hollow <u>place</u> in the <u>ground</u>. <u>Caves</u> are <u>mainly</u> naturally formed and <u>normally</u> are big enough for a person to enter. But there are also some small <u>openings</u> that we call <u>caves</u>. <u>Caves</u> provide real <u>shelters</u> when it <u>rains</u>. Each of us may hear the story about the <u>beast</u> in the <u>cave</u>. Besides <u>screaming</u>, we need to find the <u>road</u> to <u>lead</u> us out of the <u>cave</u> then.

洞穴就是地面上陷下去的地方。洞穴大都是自然形成的，通常都大到人们可以进入。但是我们所谓的洞穴，还包括一些小开口的。下雨时洞穴真的能提供给我们真正的庇护。我们每个人大概都听过关于洞穴中猛兽的故事。那时候除了尖叫外，我们必须找出能让我们逃出洞口的道路。

Unit 5 双元音 [aɪ]、[aʊ]、[ɔɪ]

Lesson 1 的发音课最后，我们要学习双元音 [aɪ]、[aʊ]、[ɔɪ]。

♪ MP3 01-09

i、y、ie、i_e 常发双元音 [aɪ]

- side [saɪd] n 边
- die [daɪ] v 死亡
- light [laɪt] n 光线
- hire [ˈhaɪr] v 雇用
- fly [flaɪ] v 飞
- type [taɪp] n 种类 v 打字

ou、ow 常发双元音 [aʊ]

- cloud [klaʊd] n 云
- ouch [aʊtʃ] int 哎呀
- owl [aʊl] n 猫头鹰
- tower [ˈtaʊɚ] n 塔
- crowd [kraʊd] n 群众

oi、oy 常发双元音 [ɔɪ]

- coin [kɔɪn] n 硬币
- voice [vɔɪs] n 声音
- annoy [əˈnɔɪ] v 使苦恼
- toy [tɔɪ] n 玩具
- oyster [ˈɔɪstɚ] n 牡蛎

大声练习！念出下列的单词、句子和文章。

♪ MP3 01-10

- **Pie** 派
  ↓
- the **Price** of **Pie**. 派的价格。
  ↓
- The **price** of **pie** is **high**. 派的价格很高。
  ↓
- The **price** of **pie** is **high** because it is a lemon **cloud pie**.
  派的价格很高，因为它是柠檬云朵派。
  ↓
- This lemon **cloud pie** will keep your holiday **crowd** happy although the **price** is **high**.
  这个柠檬云朵派会让您的假日宾客们感到很开心，虽然价位很高。
  ↓
- This lemon **cloud pie** will keep your holiday **crowd** happy because everybody will like it although the **price** is **high**. You can make sure it is tasty enough, and you will not be **annoyed**.
  这个柠檬云朵派会让您的假日宾客们感到很开心，虽然价位很高，但是每个人都会喜欢它。您可以确定它很好吃，您不必再苦恼。

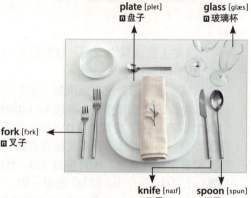

plate [plet] n 盘子
glass [glæs] n 玻璃杯
fork [fɔrk] n 叉子
knife [naɪf] n 刀子
spoon [spun] n 汤匙

🎵 MP3 01-11

Can you teach yourself to sing with a good voice? Surely, you can. Here are some tips to help you. Relax yourself first. Do not force yourself to sing the note as high as in the clouds. Do not drink iced water. You also need to practice your breathing. Don't forget to record yourself to get to know whether your singing voice gives people pleasure to listen to. Don't be afraid to practice singing in front of people. KTVs may be a good place to start your practice. Lastly, be open to criticism. Criticism helps you to know people's true reaction and thoughts.

你可以自学唱出好声音吗？当然，你可以的。这里有一些诀窍可以帮助你。首先，放轻松。不要强迫自己唱出如天一般高的高音。不要喝冰水。你必须练习呼吸。其次，别忘了录下自己的声音，这样才能知道聆听时你的歌声是否能给人愉悦感。不要害怕在人前练习。KTV是个练习的好地方。最后，要勇于接受批评。批评可以让你了解人们真正的反应和想法。

　　读完上面这篇文章后，我们就把发音规则学成了，但是……为什么大家的英语还是说不好？因为：

❶ 浊辅音跟清辅音没有搞清楚。例如，**pig** 和 **pick** 要念清楚。
❷ 该卷舌的 **r** 没有卷舌，变成 **l**。**ruler** 变成 **luler**。
❸ **m** 没有闭嘴，变成 **n**。**mama** 念成 **nana**。
❹ 发 [ð]、[θ] 音时，舌头没放在舌间。**think** 念成 **sink**。
❺ 尾音没有念清楚，**not** 变成 **no**，**top** 变成 **to**。
❻ [æ]、[ɛ]、[e]、[a] 和 [ʌ] 混成一团。
❼ 还有很重要的，英语发音规则有很多例外，像 **buy**（购买）不念 [bʌɪ]，而是念 [baɪ]；**ruin**（毁坏）不念 [run]，而是念 [ˈruɪn]。

　　要把英语念好的重点是先掌握简单的见字发音规则，把常见的规则记熟，学习每个单词前可以先用线上字典作为辅助，输入新单词让电脑念给你听，你再跟着念，念多了之后，发音对你而言就不再陌生了。

Lesson 2
一起用英语交朋友！

学习重点 1 | 用简单的英语和外国人寒暄
学习重点 2 | 用简单的句型，扩展与延伸对话
学习重点 3 | 和朋友在社群媒体上用英语聊天
学习重点 4 | 运用基本的 5W1H 句型，进行自我介绍
学习重点 5 | 活用不同句型与排列组合，让自我介绍更加丰富

Unit 1 英语会话开场白

情境是两个第一次见面的人，需要先自我介绍，然后要问对方的名字，再进行寒暄。

第一句就是告诉对方你的名字，**My name is Sally Wu.** 我是吴莎莉。
换你，把你的英语姓名放进来，**My name is _____.**

接着，告诉别人你的故乡，**I am from Beijing, China.** 我来自中国北京。
在英语中，地方名词要先说小地方，然后说大地方。所以，中文说"我来自加州"，英语就要变成：**I am from California, the USA.** 如果是美国加州的旧金山，由小到大就变成：**I am from San Francisco, California, the USA.**

介绍完自己，当然要问一下别人的名字，**What is your name?**（你叫什么名字？）
你这么问之后，如果对方是男士，就会欣然告诉你，**John、Calvin** 或 **Tom** 等名字，如果对方是女士，那么答案就会是 **Apple、Betty** 或 **Cammy**。

听完别人的姓名后，跟着讲一遍，把后面的尾音拉长，变成给对方提问题，**Tom?**（是汤姆吗？）其实在这里提出问题非常恰当，一来证明你跟对方有互动，你在听；二来也可以加深你对对方姓名的印象。所以，我们来练习一下，可以放进去所有的英语姓名，**Calvin? John? Betty?**（凯文？约翰？贝蒂？）

紧接着，就说你们见面寒暄的最重要一句："很高兴跟你见面！"**Nice to meet you!**）如果对方讲完他/她的名字后，马上先讲了这句，**Nice to meet you!** 你也别怕，我们有对策的，你就加上 **too**，变成 **Nice to meet you, too.**（我也很高兴见到你。）

对话情境

♪ MP3 02-01

A: My name is Sally Wu. I am from Beijing, China.
B: Hi, Sally.
A: What's your name*?
B: Tom.
A: Tom? Nice to meet* you.

A：我是吴莎莉。我来自中国北京。
B：嗨，莎莉。
A：你叫什么名字？
B：汤姆。
A：汤姆？很高兴见到你。

以这短短的六个句子作为开始，我们学习到 A is B "**主语加上 be 动词再加上表语**"的简单句型，记住 **My name is Sally Wu.** 在这里 A = B。我的名字就是吴莎莉。

为了让大家熟悉这种简单的句型，我们再来看看在自我介绍中如何使用这个简单的句型。

实用句型

am _____ .
我是 _____ 。

I am a mother.
我是位母亲。（表示身份）

→ 还可以用：**grandfather**（祖父）、**grandmother**（祖母）、**daughter**（女儿）、**son**（儿子）……等

I am a teacher.
我是个老师。（表示职业）

→ 还可以用：**student**（学生）、**clerk**（职员）、**officer**（上班族）、**agent**★（中介、代理）、**police**（警察）、**doctor**（医生）、**driver**（司机）……

I am a college graduate★.
我是大学毕业生。（表示学历）

I am a book lover★.
我爱看书。（表示兴趣）

I am the eldest★ **child in my family.**
我是家中的老大。（表示排行）

▶ 大声读出这些句型，你也可以使用其他词如 **father**（父亲）、**student**（学生）、**high school graduate**（高中毕业生）、**sports lover**（运动爱好者）和 **the youngest child**（老幺）来做替换。

单词补充 ♪ MP3 02-02
★ **name** [nem] n 名字
★ **meet** [mit] v 认识、遇见
★ **agent** ['edʒənt] n 中介、代理商
★ **graduate** ['grædʒʊɪt] n 大学毕业生
　　　　　　 ['grædʒʊet] v 毕业
★ **lover** ['lʌvɚ] n 爱好者、情人
★ **eldest** ['ɛldɪst]
　 adj 最年长的（**old** 的最高级）

Unit 2 用来持续对话的句型

如果你想要多了解一下和你谈话的人，你可以使用下列几个简单的句型来继续谈话！

对于第一次见面的人又处在一个陌生的环境，最好与最安全的问题就是问他／她 **Is this your first time here?**（你第一次到这里吗？）

不管答案是什么，你接着就可以问 **Do you enjoy your time here?**（你在这里愉快吗？）

出于礼貌，对方会说些好话，你也可以礼貌地回复 **Great! You must have a lot of fun.**（太棒了！你一定玩得很开心。）

你如果想询问对方做什么工作，就可以说 **What do you do?**（你做什么工作？）记得千万不要跟 **How do you do?**（你好吗？）这种与陌生人第一次见面的问好用语搞混了！

对方说完他／她的工作后，你可以回应 **It sounds interesting!**（听起来很有趣！）

学会了这些简单句型后，我们来看一下使用这些句型的完整对话情境。

对话情境　　　　　　　　　　　　　♪ MP3 02-03

Ⓐ: Is this your first time here?

Ⓑ: Yes, this is my first time here at this university*.

Ⓐ: Do you enjoy your time here?

Ⓑ: I do, and thank you.

Ⓐ: Great! You must have a lot of* fun. What do you do?

Ⓑ: I am a designer*.

Ⓐ: It sounds interesting.

A：你第一次来这里吗？

B：是啊，我第一次来这个大学。

A：你喜欢这里吗？

B：我喜欢，谢谢！

A：太好了，你一定很开心。你做什么工作？

B：我是个设计师。

A：听起来很有趣。

NOTICE!

练习了完整的对话后,你轻轻松松就学会了可以持续对话三分钟的约二十个英语句型,我们再来利用已经学习到的作为基础来延伸学习。

除了 "Great" "太棒了"、"interesting" "有趣的" 之类的形容词之外,下面也是外国人常用来形容太好了、太赞了与棒极了的常见形容词。

常用于表达不可置信的惊喜
- **amazing** [əˈmezɪŋ] a 惊人的
- **exciting** [ɪkˈsaɪtɪŋ] a 令人兴奋的
- **fascinating** [ˈfæsn̩ˌetɪŋ] a 迷人的

较口语的用法
- **cool** [kul] a 很棒的
- **perfect** [ˈpɜfɪkt] a 完美的
- **wonderful** [ˈwʌndɚfəl] a 极好的
- **terrific** [təˈrɪfɪk] a 了不起的

常用于职场上
- **magnificent** [mægˈnɪfəsənt] a 宏伟的
- **decent** [ˈdisnt] a 合乎礼仪的
- **awesome** [ˈɔsəm] a 令人惊叹的

负面的用法
- **terrible** [ˈtɛrəbl] a 可怕的
- **horrible** [ˈhɔrəbl] a 可怕的
- **awful** [ˈɔful] a 吓人的
- **bad** [bæd] a 不好的

会话补充 Conversation ♪ MP3 02-04

A: I am a cook*.
B: It sounds cool.
A: Yes, I love my job.
A: I work for a mean* real estate* agent.
B: It sounds terrible.
A: I couldn't agree with you more.

A:我是厨师。
B:听起来很酷。
A:对啊,我爱我的工作。
A:我在一个苛刻的房屋中介所工作。
B:听起来很糟糕。
A:我不能同意你更多。

单词补充 ♪ MP3 02-05

★ **university** [junəˈvɜsəti] n 大学
★ **a lot of** pn 许多、大量
★ **designer** [dɪˈzaɪnɚ] n 设计师
★ **cook** [kuk] n 厨师 v 煮
★ **mean** [min] a 苛刻的、吝啬的
★ **real estate** pn 不动产

社群媒体中的英语对话

学了句型，也背了单词，我们就利用社交软件来练习一下之前学的句型，以下是莎莉跟安德鲁两个初次认识的人在 **skype** 上的对话。

♪ MP3 02-06

接下来，换你上 **skype**、**line** 跟 **facebook** 等社群媒体找个人来聊天练习英语了！

你有没有注意到，从一开始的短句到现在，我们已经把英语句子慢慢拉长了，要把你的英语句子拉长，我们就要学习使用连接词。

语法教室

什么是连接词？连接词跟糨糊一样是用来连接用的，连接词主要有三种，有对等连接词、从属连接词和连接副词，可以用来连接"单词""短语"和"从句"。先来看对等连接词，如粉丝男孩们（FANBOYS）。

对等连接词（粉丝男孩─FANBOYS）

For	**A**nd	**N**or	**B**ut	**O**r	**Y**et	**S**o
因为	和	也不、也不是	但是	或	然而	所以

我们来看看怎么使用"粉丝男孩们"！因为"粉丝男孩们"是对等连接词，所以只能连接同样的事物，所以连接原则必须是：

❶ （词性相同）单词 ＋ 对等连接词 ＋（词性相同）单词

We celebrate* her birthday with <u>cakes</u>, <u>flowers</u> and <u>snacks</u>. ⟶ 连接名词
我们使用蛋糕、鲜花及点心来庆祝她的生日。

<u>He</u> is not allowed* to talk to strangers, neither am <u>I</u>. ⟶ 连接代名词
他不允许和陌生人说话，我也是。
注意 使用 neither 皆不时，助动词得放在前面形成倒装句。

He is <u>old</u> but <u>wise</u>*. ⟶ 连接形容词
他年纪大，但是很有智慧。

❷ （词性相同）短语 ＋ 对等连接词 ＋（词性相同）短语

Would you like to go <u>in the morning</u> or <u>in the afternoon</u>? ⟶ 连接表示时间的介词短语
你要早上去还是下午去？

❸ 从句 ＋ 对等连接词 ＋ 从句

For <u>I am a teacher</u>, <u>I go to school every day</u>. ⟶ 连接从句
因为我是老师，我每天去学校。

<u>It is a good film</u>, yet <u>there is age limit</u>*. ⟶ 连接两个从句
这是部好片，但是有年龄限制。

<u>The weather</u>* is going to get chilly tonight, so <u>we need to bring big coats</u>. ⟶ 连接两个从句
今晚天气会变冷，所以我们必须带厚外套。

接着就是实际使用 **FANBOYS** 来拉长句子,以下的范例使用 **FANBOYS** 的对等连接词来介绍我或你会说的语言。

♪ MP3 02-07

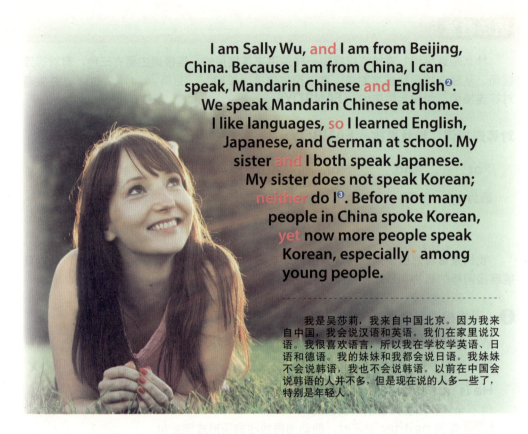

I am Sally Wu, and I am from Beijing, China. Because I am from China, I can speak, Mandarin Chinese and English❷. We speak Mandarin Chinese at home. I like languages, so I learned English, Japanese, and German at school. My sister and I both speak Japanese. My sister does not speak Korean; neither do I❸. Before not many people in China spoke Korean, yet now more people speak Korean, especially* among young people.

我是吴莎莉,我来自中国北京。因为我来自中国,我会说汉语和英语。我们在家里说汉语。我很喜欢语言,所以我在学校学英语、日语和德语。我的妹妹和我都会说日语。我妹妹不会说韩语,我也不会说韩语。以前在中国会说韩语的人并不多,但是现在说的人多一些了,特别是年轻人。

实用句型

❶ I am really happy to _____ .

我真的很高兴_____。

❷ I can speak _____, _____, and _____ .

我会说_____、_____和_____。

注意 and 放在最后一项事物之前。

❸ My sister does not _____ , neither do I.

我妹妹不会_____,我也是。

单词补充 ♪ MP3 02-08

★ **engineer** [ˌɛndʒəˈnɪr] n 工程师
★ **translator** [trænsˈletɚ] n 译者
★ **celebrate** [ˈsɛləbret] v 庆祝
★ **allow** [əˈlaʊ] v 允许
★ **wise** [waɪz] a 聪明的
★ **limit** [ˈlɪmɪt] n v 限制
★ **weather** [ˈwɛðɚ] n 天气
★ **especially** [əˈspɛʃəlɪ] ad 特别、尤其

Unit 4 来场简单的自我介绍

下一个情境是 5 个 W 加上一个 H 的问句句型在谈话中的使用。　♪ MP3 02-09

Who（谁）
Q: Who am I?
我是谁？
A: I am Sally Wu, a teacher.
我是吴莎莉，是位老师。

When（何时）
Q: When did you come?
你什么时候来的？
A: I came about five minutes ago.
我五分钟前来的。

What（什么）
Q: What do you do?
你做哪一行？
A: I am a store clerk.
我是店员。

Where（何地）
Q: Where are you going this weekend?
你这星期打算去哪？
A: I am planning to go to the park.
我打算去公园。

Why（原因）
Q: Why were you late?
你为什么迟到？
A: I was late because I went to see a doctor.
我迟到是因为去看医生了。

How（程度、方法）
Q: How's the weather today?
今天天气如何？
A: It's nice.
不错。

Q: How did you arrive?
你怎么来的？
A: I arrived by high speed rail.
我坐高铁来的。

答句中画线的地方是 5 个 WH + 1 个 How 的答案关键词。举例来说，别人问你 Who are you? 你不需要详细回答"I am..."，但一定要告知你的姓名和身份，像是例句中的"Sally Wu, a teacher."

另外，5WH + 1How 也可以帮助你提升听力。当问题是 What 时，你就专心听事物；当问题是 Why 时，就听原因。善加利用 5 个 WH + 1 个 How 句型，英语的听说读写就可以突飞猛进。

接下来的情境，我们就利用 5 个 WH+1 个 How 句型先拟出问句，然后来篇短短的自我介绍。

问题为：

❶ **Who am I?** 我是谁？
❷ **What do I do?** 我做什么？
❸ **Where do I come from?** 我来自哪里？
❹ **What is my motto?** 我的格言是什么？
❺ **Why do I believe in my motto?** 我为什么相信我的格言？
❻ **How do I feel about myself?** 我怎样看待自己？

上述问题的答案如下：

I am a young officer. I am a computer engineer. I come from a small family, and my motto is "Nothing Is Impossible." With the love and support of my family and friends, I believe nothing is impossible. I feel truly good about myself.

我是位年轻的上班族。我是电脑工程师。我来自一个小家庭，我的格言是"没有不可能的事"。有我的家人和朋友的爱与支持，我相信没有不可能的事。我觉得自己很棒。

你看，一下子你会了 56 个词的自我介绍。在此也介绍一个可以增加篇幅与长度的方法，你可以把 5WH+1 How 的问句放进去做自我介绍，效果也不错。范例如下：

(Who am I?) I am a young office worker. (What do I do?) I am a computer engineer. (Where do I come from?) I come from a small family, and I live with my parents and one sister. (What is my motto?) My motto is "Nothing Is Impossible." Why is that? With the love and support of my families and friends, I believe nothing is impossible. (How do I feel about myself?) I feel truly good about myself.

（我是谁？）我是位年轻的上班族。（我做什么工作？）我是电脑工程师。（我来自何处？）我来自一个小家庭，我和父母亲及一个妹妹住一起。（我的格言是什么？）我的格言是"没有不可能的事"。为什么？有我的家人和朋友的爱与支持，我相信没有不可能的事。（我如何看待自己？）我觉得自己很棒。

▶ 你可以把问题放进你的自我介绍中来加强对方对你的注意，但是切记，不要使用两个以上的问句，否则听起来就很像在"碎碎念"。

▶ 记几个又简单、又实用的格言，不仅可以励志，也可以在自我介绍和交谈中使用！
Take action. 采取行动。
Do my best! 尽我所能！
Never give up. 永不放弃！
Life is a choice. 人生就是个选择。

Unit 5 使自我介绍的内容更加丰富

除了 5WH + 1How 的句子以外，英语中还有其他句型，都可以让你的自我介绍更出色。接下来利用上个 unit 学过的格言来做变化：

- **I believe in love.** 我相信爱。（肯定陈述）
- **I am not a naive person.** 我不是个天真的人。（**be** 动词加 **not** 的否定陈述）
- **I will not sit still.** 我不会坐以待毙。（助动词加上 **not** 的否定陈述）
- **Is life a choice?** 生命是个选择？（**Yes / No** 疑问句）
- **Should I do my best or give up?** 我要尽我所能还是放弃呢？（选择性疑问句）
- **Take action to love what I believe.** 采取行动爱我所相信的事物。（祈使句）
- **We never never never give up, shouldn't we?** 我们应该永不放弃，不是吗？（附加疑问句）
- **Can you tell me what I should do?** 你是否能够告诉我我该做什么？（间接疑问句，**Can you tell me** + 5 个 **wh** + 1 个 **how** 疑问词 + 主语 + 动词？）

这些都可以放在自我介绍中，来看看下列的排列组合的例子。你当然可以有不同的排列组合方式，变动一下这些句子的顺序，会有不同的感觉。

自我介绍 🎵 MP3 02-10

I am not a naive person. I believe ＊ in love. Take action to love what I believe. I will not sit still. Is life a choice? Can you tell me what I should do? We never never never give up, shouldn't we? Should I do my best or give up?

我不是个天真的人。我相信爱。采取行动，爱我所相信的事物。我不会坐以待毙。生命是个选择吗？你是否能够告诉我我该做什么？我们应该永不放弃，不是吗？我要尽我所能还是放弃呢？

在描述人格时，有好多形容词可以使用，我们分别来看描述人格优缺点的形容词。

优点
- active [ˈæktɪv] 主动的、积极的
- friendly [ˈfrɛndlɪ] 友善的
- polite [pəˈlaɪt] 有礼貌的
- smart [smɑrt] 聪明的
- tough [tʌf] 坚强的

缺点
- passive [ˈpæsɪv] 被动的
- lazy [ˈlezɪ] 懒散的
- sensitive [ˈsɛnsətɪv] 敏感的
- shy [ʃaɪ] 害羞的
- impatient [ɪmˈpeʃənt] 没耐心的

语法教室

a _____ person 或 an _____ person 的差别就在于你选用的形容词是否为 a、e、i、o、u 等元音发音，像 an important person （重要的人）或 an impatient person （没耐心的人）。

元音是 a、e、i、o、u！

实用句型

初阶版

❶ I am a / an _____ person.
我是个 _____ 的人。

I am an active person. 我是个主动的人。

I am a polite. 我是个有礼貌的人。

❷ Most of my friends would say I am a / an _____ person.
我的朋友大多认为我是个 _____ 的人。

Most of my friends would say I am a sensitive person.
我的朋友大多认为我是个敏感的人。

Most of my friends would say I am an impatient person.
我的朋友大多认为我是个没耐心的人。

进阶版 自我介绍会决定别人对你的第一印象，而第一印象只有一个，所以很重要的是要记得把缺点说清楚，并将它变成优点，怎么做呢？

❶ I am a / an _____ person.
我是个 _____ 的人。

I am a passive person. I spend most of my time learning from others.
我是个被动的人。我花很多时间向别人学习。

I am a shy person. I always observe* at the beginning*.
我是个害羞的人。我一开始都先观察。

❷ Most of my friends would say I am a / an _____ person.
我的朋友大多认为我是个 _____ 的人。

Most of my friends think I am a sensitive person. I really care about others.
我的朋友大多认为我是个敏感的人。我真的很在乎其他人。

介绍家人在自我介绍中也很重要，接下来看一篇介绍家庭成员的对话。

对话情境

♪ MP3 02-11

A: How many people are there in your family?

B: I am from an extensive* family. There are nine people in my family.

A: Do you have any siblings?

B: Yes, I have two sisters and two brothers.

A: Are your brothers and sisters younger or older than you?

B: I am the eldest child in the family. They are my younger brothers and sisters.

A：你家有多少人？

B：我来自一个大家庭，家中有九个人。

A：你有兄弟姐妹吗？

B：是的，我有两个妹妹和两个弟弟。

A：你的兄弟姐妹比你大还是小？

B：我是老大，他们都是弟弟和妹妹。

如果要把对话改成自我陈述的介绍，范例如下：

♪ MP3 02-12

Hello, I am <u>Alex</u>. I am from a <u>big</u> family. There are <u>nine</u> people in my family. They are my <u>grandparents</u>, my <u>parents</u>, my <u>sisters</u> and <u>brothers</u>, and me. I am the <u>eldest</u> child in the family. I have <u>two younger</u> brothers and sisters.

你好，我是艾力克斯。我来自一个大家庭，家中有九个人，有祖父母、父母、兄弟姐妹和我。我是老大，我还有两个弟弟和两个妹妹。

▶ 画线的单词，可以替换成符合自己家庭状况的信息。
▶ 如果是独生子女，就说：I am the only child in the family. I have no brothers and sisters.（我是家里唯一的小孩，我没有兄弟姐妹。）

接下来，补充说明在讨论到家庭关系时，会用到的单词：

grandparents 祖父母	grandfather 祖父 grandpa 祖父	grandmother 祖母 grandma 祖母
parents 父母	father 父亲	mother 母亲
siblings 兄弟姐妹	elder brother 哥哥 elder sister 姐姐	younger brother 弟弟 younger sister 妹妹
relative 亲戚	uncle 叔伯 cousin 表兄弟姐妹	aunt 姑婶
family 家庭	big family 大家庭 extensive family 大家庭	small family 小家庭 nuclear family 小家庭

爱好，可以让别人更了解你，可以因爱好而成为朋友。 ♪MP3 02-13

In my free* time, I like stamp collecting. I am interested in collecting stamps from all over the world. I also like traveling. I don't have time and money for it. By collecting stamps, I get to know the world better. It also helps me to relax* myself.

我空闲时喜欢集邮，我对来自全世界各地的邮票感兴趣。我也喜欢旅游，但是没有时间和金钱。集邮让我更了解这个世界，也帮助我放松。

▶ 画线的单词，可以把自己喜欢的爱好填进去。补充常见的爱好单词，如下：

运动 basketball（篮球）、baseball（棒球）、tennis（网球）、table tennis（乒乓球）、badminton（羽毛球）

文艺 singing（唱歌）、dancing（跳舞）、playing chess（象棋）、wine tasting（品酒）

室内 playing computer games（电脑游戏）、stamp collecting（集邮）、sewing（缝纫）、cooking（烹饪）

户外 traveling（旅游）、gardening（园艺）、hiking（徒步旅行）

会话补充 Conversation ♪MP3 02-14

A: What do you like doing?
B: In my free time, I like stamp collecting.

A: 你喜欢做什么？
B: 我喜欢集邮。

A: What hobbies do you have?
B: I relax by playing computer games.

A: 你有什么爱好？
B: 我喜欢打电脑游戏放松自己。

单词补充 ♪MP3 02-15

★ believe [bɪˈliv] v 相信、信任
★ observe [əbˈzɝv] v 观察
★ beginning [bɪˈgɪnɪŋ] n 开始、开端
★ extensive [ɪkˈstɛnsɪv] a 庞大的
★ free [fri] a 空闲的
★ relax [rɪˈlæks] v 放松

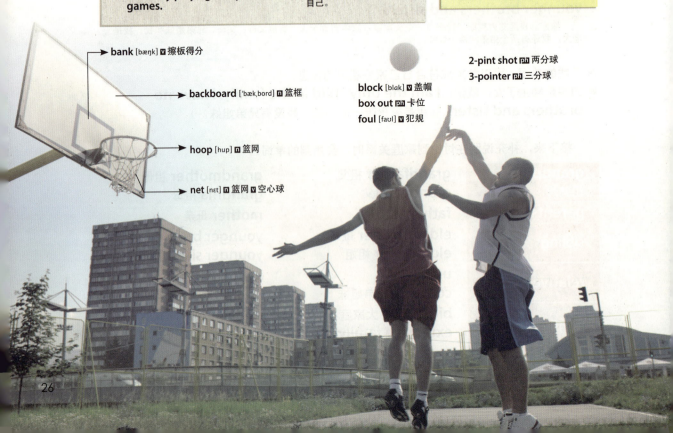

bank [bæŋk] v 擦板得分
backboard [ˈbækˌbord] n 篮框
hoop [hup] n 篮网
net [nɛt] n 篮网 v 空心球

block [blɑk] v 盖帽
box out ph 卡位
foul [faʊl] v 犯规

2-pint shot ph 两分球
3-pointer ph 三分球

Unit 1 在职场上主动出击

首先，想想看，我们在工作中做什么时会使用英语？E-mail！不管是被动等客户来询价，还是主动出击介绍公司，你都需要使用英语来写 E-mail！

实用单词

MP3 03-01

availability [əˌveləˈbɪlətɪ] n 可以购买的产品
inquire [ɪnˈkwaɪr] v 询问
catalog [ˈkætəlɔg] n 目录
website [ˈwɛb,saɪt] n 网站
quantity [ˈkwantətɪ] n 数量
quality [ˈkwalətɪ] n 品质
price list ph 价目表
offer [ˈɔfɚ] v 报价

在职场上，收到的 E-mail 如下，请留意画线部分的句型：

| To | |
| Subject: | |

　　I am writing to❶ inquire about the availability of Product ABC. I have seen the product details * on your website, and I'm very interested in❷ getting to know more about your products. I will appreciate very much if you could❸ send me samples, so I can❹ test before making a decision. I have confidence in❻ your products, but the procurement process of our company requires tests before any purchase. I will also appreciate if you could❺ send me the price list bulk purchasing. I need to take a decision in the coming few days for next quarter's * purchase, so it's very important that❼ I receive this information as soon as possible. Look forward to❽ your timely reply.

Best regards,

Frank Msiller
Sales Manager of DEF

　　我写这封邮件是要询问有关 ABC 产品的购买事宜。我在网站上看到你们产品的目录，我很感兴趣，想要更多了解你们的产品。如果你们可以寄给我一些样品，让我可以在决定采购前进行测试，我很感激。我对你们的产品有信心，但是我们公司的采购流程规定在购买前必须做测试。如果你们能寄给我大量购买的折扣价目表，我也会非常感激。我在未来几天必须做出下一季的采购决定，因此必须尽快收到相关信息。期待你们的尽快回复。

致敬

法兰克·米勒
DEF 公司销售经理

注意 信的结尾都要附上 Best regards 或 Yours sincerely, Yours faithfully 致敬等，也要有姓名和职称，如 Frank Miller, Sales Manager of DEF（法兰克·米勒，DEF 公司销售经理）。

Lesson 3

问题是收到这样的邮件，要怎么回复呢？

To:
Subject:

❶ 很简单，首先我们要简单地谢谢对方的回复。

❷ 然后，告知对方你已经了解了对方的用意并且已经在处理。

❸ 告知对方目前 ABC 产品的状态。

❹ 回复有关样品及大宗购买折扣价。

❺ 通知对方报价在你的邮件附件中。

❻ 希望你提供的信息对潜在客户有帮助。

❼ 最后礼貌地询问对方是否需要提供进一步的服务。

❽ 别忘了邮件的结尾。

❶ Dear Mr. Miller,
Thank you for your email on December 28, 2015. ❷ Your inquiry has been well received and handled. ❸ We now have Product ABC available in stock*. ❹ We have sent you the samples that you requested this morning, and quantity discount* prices are offered for bulk purchasing of 5,000 pieces and more. ❺ In the attachment you can find the price list of our products including both retailing and bulk purchasing*.
❻ Hopefully, we have served your needs and helped you to make the decision on purchase. ❼ If you need any further help, please do not hesitate to contact us. Look forward to building the long-term* business relationship with your company.
❽ Yours sincerely,
Rita Wu
Sales Director of 0101 Company

---

❶ 米勒先生您好：
感谢您 2015 年 12 月 28 日的邮件。❷ 我们已经收到您的询问并且已经处理。
❸ 我们目前有 ABC 产品的库存。❹ 我们已经在今天早上寄出了您要求的商品，大宗购买的折扣价格是提供给购买 5000 件以上的客户的。❺ 附件有我们的产品价目表，包括零售与大宗购买的价格。
❻ 希望我们已经提供的您所需的资料能帮助您做出采购决定。❼ 如果您需要进一步的协助，请马上跟我们联络。期待与您的公司建立长期的商务关系。

❽ 致敬

吴瑞塔
0101 公司销售主任

单词补充 ♪ MP3 03-02

★ **details** ['ditel] n 细节
★ **quarter** ['kwɔrtɚ] n 季度
★ **in stock** ph 有现货、有库存
★ **discount** ['dɪskaʊnt] v 打折
★ **bulk purchasing** ph 大宗购买
★ **long-term** ['lɔŋ,tɝm] a 长期的

不可不知的办公室电话

有一件有趣的事，可以跟大家分享。在一家与南亚地区有生意往来的公司中，助理因为英语不好，只能用标准操作程序 SOP 来接听南亚地区的客户电话，那个 SOP 就是，寒暄、礼貌性地确认来电者身份，然后告知对方请用邮件确认要联系的事项，然后挂上电话。这个 SOP 每次都能帮助助理顺利地接听完英语电话。

一般而言，电话交谈可以分成三个部分：寒暄、主旨和结尾等。所使用的英语句型也很固定，所以很简单、易学，赶快学起来！

♪ MP3 03-03

寒暄

Good morning / Good afternoon / Good evening
早安 / 午安 / 晚安
Hello 嗨
ABC Company ABC 公司
How can I help you? May I help you?
需要我为您服务吗？有什么可为您效劳的？

一拿起电话，您就可以马上用英语说：
Good morning, ABC Company. This is Sally. How can I help you?
早安，这里是 ABC 公司。我是莎莉。有什么可为您服务的？
或者是：
Good afternoon, ABC Company. This is Sally. May I help you?
下午好，这里是 ABC 公司。我是莎莉。有什么可为您服务的？

主旨

说完后，对方会说明打电话来的主要用意，我们就进入电话的第二部分主旨了。对方可能会说：
This is Ronald Factor, calling from DEF.
我是雷纳德斐克特，DEF 公司打来的。
I am looking for Ms. Wu. 我要找吴小姐。

这里的重点在于要听清楚对方的姓名，哪个公司打来的以及要找谁。还记得 Lesson 2 学过的技巧吗？**Ronald Factor?**（雷纳德斐克特？）可以使用提高语调的方法来确认姓名与名称！
如果拼不出来姓名或名称，就大方地问，**How to spell?** 或 **How do you spell it?**（怎么拼写？）也可以问 **Could you spell your name, please?**（请拼写出您的大名？）

获得这些信息后，你可以就以下情况来处理这个电话：

30

[如果来电者要找的人在，可以立即转接]
One moment, please! 请等一等！

I will transfer* your call to Ms. Wu.
I will connect* you to Ms. Wu. 我将您的电话转给吴小姐。

Her extension* number is 0123. 她的分机是 0123
I will get her. 我请她来听电话。

[如果来电者要找的人不在]
Sorry. / I am sorry. 抱歉。/ 我很抱歉。

Ms. Wu is not available* now. 吴小姐，现在不在。
Ms. Wu is at the meeting now. 吴小姐现在在开会。
Ms. Wu is on another line. 她在接听别的电话。

I will transfer your call to someone who can help you.
我把您的电话转给可以协助您的人。
Would you please hold? 您可以稍等下吗？

如果对方没时间等或一定得跟吴小姐讲电话。你就必须说：
May I take a message*? 我可以为您留言吗？

问完后对方可能给的信息为：
- **Yes, please ask Ms. Wu to call me back at 0912345678.**
  是的，请她回电，我的电话是 0912345678。
- **Yes, tell her Tommy from DEF called.**
  是的，告诉她 DEF 公司的汤米来过电话。
- **Yes, tell her we will meet at XYZ Café tomorrow at 12:00.**
  是的，跟她说我们明天 12:00 在 XYZ 咖啡厅见。
- **Yes, tell her to quote* me the prices of Product 0123.**
  是的，请她提供给我 0123 产品的报价。
- **Yes, tell her I will arrive* at the airport at 8:00 tomorrow morning. My flight number is AB-11.**
  是的，请告诉她我明天早上八点抵达机场。我的航班号码是 AB-11。

结 尾 在电话的结尾，要确认信息并向对方道别。
I will give her your message. 我会将您的留言交给她。
Thank you for calling. 谢谢您的来电。
Bye bye. 再见。

注意要重点听，如上面标示的，人名、地名、时间、品名和航班。

对话情境

🎵 MP3 03-04

A: Good morning, ABC Company. This is Sally. How can I help you?

B: Yes, I am Ronald Factor calling for Ms. Wu from DEF.

A: I will connect your call to her. Can you spell your name, please?

B: F-a-c-t-o-r.

A: F-a-c-t-o-r. One moment please.

B: Thank you.

A: Sorry, Mr. Factor. Ms. Wu is not available now. Can I take your message?

B: Yes, tell her to call me back at 0912345678.

A: I will give your message to her. Thank you for calling, Mr. Factor. Bye bye.

A: 早上好，ABC 公司。我是莎莉。有什么可为您服务的？

B: 是的。我是 DEF 的雷纳德斐克特，我要找吴小姐。

A: 我把您的电话转给她。可以拼出您的名字吗？

B: F-a-c-t-o-r。

A: F-a-c-t-o-r。请稍等。

B: 谢谢。

A: 不好意思，斐克特先生。吴小姐现在不在。我可以为您留言吗？

B: 可以，请她回电，我的电话是 0912345678。

A: 我会将您的留言交给她。谢谢您的来电，斐克特先生。再见。

※ 多重复几次对方姓名，除了可以多次确认，也可以让对方感觉你很有礼貌。

会话补充 Conversation 🎵 MP3 03-05

A: Hi, I'm looking for Mr. Lin.
B: I am sorry, Mr. Lin is at a meeting now. May I take a message?
A: No, that's okay. I'll try again later.

A: Hi, this is Lisa, calling from ABC company. Can you transfer to Dennis?
B: One moment, please. Sorry, Dennis is on another line. May I take a message?
A: Yes, can you tell Dennis that Lisa called?
B: Hold on, let me grab a pen and a paper. Okay, what's your number again?
A: He can reach me at 1234-5678. Thanks.

A: 嗨，我要找林先生。
A: 不好意思，林先生现在在开会。我可以帮您留言吗？
A: 没关系，我等一会再打。

A: 嗨，我是 ABC 公司的丽莎，可以帮我转接丹尼斯吗？
B: 请稍等。不好意思，丹尼斯正在打电话，我可以帮您留言吗？
A: 好的，您可以跟丹尼斯说我打来过吗？
B: 稍等一下，我拿一下纸笔。好的，可以再请您留一下电话吗？
A: 他可以打 1234-5678 找我。谢谢！

单词补充 🎵 MP3 03-06

★ **transfer** [trænsˈfɝ] ⓥ 转换、转接
★ **connect** [kəˈnɛkt] ⓥ 联络、接通电话
★ **extension** [ɪkˈstɛnʃən] ⓝ 电话分机
★ **available** [əˈveləbl] ⓐ 有空的
★ **message** [ˈmɛsɪdʒ] ⓝ 信息
★ **quote** [kwot] ⓥ/ⓝ 报价
★ **arrive** [əˈraɪv] ⓥ 到达

Unit 3 用英语接待外国客户

在工作场合中，都需要迎来送往，接下来我们学习，你在机场迎接一位客人所需要使用的社交英语。

在机场，拿着牌子，上面写着你没见过面的客人的大名：**Mr. Aaron Thomas**（亚伦托马斯先生）。然后，您的客人走出来，指着你的牌子，没错，你的客人就是他。你可以说：
Good morning! 早安。
You must be Mr. Aaron Thomas. 您一定是亚伦托马斯先生。
It's nice to meet you. 很高兴见到您。

你的这几句话对方会有什么回应呢？我们来看一下完整的对话情境。

对话情境 ♪ MP3 03-07

A: Good morning! — A：早安。
B: Good morning to you! — B：您也早。
A: You must be Mr. Aaron Thomas. — A：您一定是亚伦托马斯先生。
B: Yes, I am Aaron Thomas. — B：是的，我是亚伦托马斯。
A: It's nice to meet you. — A：很高兴见到您。
B: And you. — B：我也很高兴见到您。
A: We've been long looking forward to your visit.❶ — A：长久以来，我们一直很期待您的莅临。
B: So have I. — B：我也是。
A: May I take your luggage*? — A：我可以帮您拿行李吗？
B: Sure, and thank you. — B：好的，谢谢您。
A: Our driver and car are waiting outside, and please follow me. This way, please. — A：我们的司机和车都在外面等着，请跟我来。这边请。

上车后，抵达公司之前，中间这段时间，总不能跟你的外国客人沉默以对，这时候你能说什么呢？记住下面几句话，你就可以跟客人聊天了。
How's your trip? 您的旅程还好吗？
You must be tired. 您一定很累了！
You can take some rest. 您可以休息一下。

33

对话情境 🎵 MP3 03-08

A: How's your trip, Mr. Thomas?

B: Good but long, thank you.

A: You must be tired now.

B: Indeed.

A: It's about a 30-minute drive from the airport to our office.❷ You can take a rest.

B: Ok, and thank you.

A：您的旅途还顺利吗，托马斯先生？
B：还不错，但是旅途很长，谢谢。
A：您一定累坏了。
B：确实。
A：从机场到我们办公室约为30分钟。您可以休息一下。
B：好的，谢谢。

对话情境 🎵 MP3 03-09

A: How's your trip, Mr. Thomas?

B: Pretty good, and the flight was good.

A: You must be tired now.

B: After a cup of coffee, I fell refreshed*.

A: If you are not too exhausted, let me introduce* you some of the buildings on our way to the office.

B: Ok, and thank you.

A: On your left hand side, you will see the new shopping mall project. It is going to be completed next year. It is valued at several hundred million dollars. It will offer good opportunities for both domestic and international* investors.

B: Interesting!

A：您的旅途还顺利吗，托马斯先生？
B：不错，旅途还顺利。
A：您一定累坏了。
B：喝过咖啡后，我的精神很好。
A：如果您不是太累，让我给您介绍一下我们到办公室途中的一些建筑。
B：好的，谢谢。
A：在您左手边，您见到的是新的购物中心计划。它明年就会完成。它有数亿元的价值。它对国内和国外投资者来说都是个极佳的商机。
B：很有趣！

到了公司后，下面几句话，也都可以派上用场。　🎵 MP3 03-10

Here we are. 我们到了。
We now arrive at our headquarters office. 我们现在抵达总部大楼。
I will lead you to the meeting room. 我带您到会议室。
Our manager will introduce our company to you.
我们的经理会向您介绍我们公司。

如果你是在公司中负责接待的人员，下列的句子是你会用到的：
Hi, Mr. Thomas. 您好，托马斯先生。
Welcome to ABC Company. 欢迎来到 ABC 公司。
I am Angel. 我是安杰尔。
Let me first offer you something to drink. 让我先给您拿些喝的。
Do you prefer tea, coffee or water? 您想要喝茶、咖啡还是水呢？
Coffee will soon be served. 咖啡很快就会送上来。
How would you like to have your coffee? 您的咖啡要加牛奶还是糖？

参观完公司的后续安排，则可以使用下列几个句子：
Mr. Thomas, we will drive you to the airport around 2:00.
托马斯先生，我们在两点左右会开车带您前往机场。
We will take you back to your hotel around 4:00.
我们会在四点左右送您回到饭店。
The hotel is located at the downtown* area.
饭店就位于市中心。
Our manager has also arranged a banquet* reception for you tonight.
我们经理今晚也为您安排了晚宴。
You must visit a night market tonight. ❸
您今晚一定得到夜市看看。

实用句型

❶ **We've been long looking forward to _____ .**
长久以来，我们一直很期待 _____ 。

❷ **It's about a 30-minute drive from the _____ to _____ .**
从 _____ 到 _____ 约为 30 分钟。

❸ **You must visit _____ tonight.**
您今晚一定得到 _____ 看看。

单词补充　🎵 MP3 03-11
★ **luggage** [ˈlʌgɪdʒ] n 行李
★ **refresh** [rɪˈfrɛʃ] v 消除疲劳
★ **introduce** [ˌɪntrəˈdjus] n 介绍
★ **international** [ˌɪntɚˈnæʃən!] a 国际的
★ **downtown** [ˌdaʊnˈtaʊn] n 闹区
★ **banquet** [ˈbæŋkwɪt] n 盛会

语法教室

在 Lesson 2 中，我们学会了功能如同糨糊的 FANBOYS 对等连接词的使用方式，在这个单元，我们要继续来学习第二个连接工具：从属连接词。

我们要学习的**从属连接词**，它们是：

表示"时间先后"	before 之前、after 之后
表示"因果关系"	as 由于、because 因为
表示"条件"	if 如果、although 虽然

你一定会问为什么它们叫作从属连接词，跟之前的 FANBOYS 有什么不同？答案就是从属连接词也是糨糊，跟 FANBOYS 一样，可以用来连接两个句子，但是跟着**从属连接词的句子不可以单独存在**，跟着 **FANBOYS 的句子可以单独存在**！因为如果跟着从属连接词的句子单独存在，不只语法上不正确，而且语意上也不完整。

例如，你如果跟朋友说：
- **Before** I went to school. 我去学校之前。
- **After** I finish my dinner. 吃完我的晚餐后。
- **Because** I am tired. 因为我很累。
- **As** we are friends. 由于我们是朋友。
- **Although** she is young. 虽然她年纪很小。
- **If** it rains. 如果下雨了。

→ 说这些句子会让人觉得没有上下文，这些句子会变成"悬疑的句子"，让人摸不着头绪。正确的句子应该如下：

- **Before** I go to school, I always read newspaper.
  我去学校之前，都会先看报纸。
- **After** I finish my dinner, I will go to his home. 我吃完晚餐后，会去他家。
- I am not going to the New Year's Eve party **because** I am tired.
  我不去除夕派对，因为我很累。
- I am very happy to help you **as** we are friends.
  由于我们是朋友，我很高兴协助你。
- **Although** she is young, she is wise. 虽然她年纪很小，她很有智慧。
- I will stay home **if** it rains. 如果下雨了，我就待在家。

上述句子在语法上是正确的，语意上也更完整。此外，还要提醒你两件事：
❶ 从属连接词可以依据语意放在句首或中间。
❷ 如果从属连接词放在中间，前面不可以放逗号。

注意看看上面几个从属连接词放在中间的句子，都没有逗号！比较一下以下两组分别使用 for 和 because，表达"我不去除夕派对，因为我很累。"的句子。

对等连接词 for（因为）

For I am tired, I am not going to the New Year's Eve party.

I am not going to the New Year's Eve party, for I am tired.

从属连接词 because（因为）

Because I am tired, I am not going to the New Year's Eve party.

I am not going to the New Year's Eve party because I am tired.

注意 对等连接词，放在中间位置，前面必须有逗号，从属连接词放在中间，前面不可以有逗号。

使用从属连接词要如何来连接下列句子呢？
- On your left hand side, you will see the new shopping mall project.
  在您左手边，您见到的是新的购物中心计划。
- It represents the value of several hundred million dollars. 它有数亿元的价值。
- It will give good opportunities for both domestic and international investors. 它对国内和国外投资者来说都是个极佳的商机。

❶ 表示时间先后的 after（之后）

After it is completed, it represents the value of several hundred million dollars. 它完成后代表着数亿元的价值。

❷ 表示因果关系的：as（由于）

It will give good opportunities for both domestic and international investors as it represents the value of several hundred million dollars. 由于它代表着数亿元的价值，对国内和国外投资者来说都是个极佳的商机。

❸ 表示条件的：although（虽然）

Although this is a new shopping mall project, it presents the value of several hundred million dollars. 虽然这是个新的购物中心计划，它却有数亿元的价值。

从小我们就常用"虽然……但是……"造句，英语中的 although（虽然）可以单独使用，但如果要用英语表达"虽然……但是……"，其中的"但是……"，只能使用 yet，不可以用 but，所以正确的句子为：

Although this is a new shopping mall project, it represents the value of several hundred million dollars.

Although this is a new shopping mall project, yet it represents the value of several hundred million dollars.

虽然这是个新的购物中心计划，但是它却有数亿元的价值。

Unit 4 每到佳节必问候

岁末年终，我们都要写张圣诞和新年卡片给往来的外国客户，有些吉祥话是我们也要学的英语。

从简单的开始，你当然可以写上 **Merry Christmas**（圣诞快乐）、**Happy New Year**（新年快乐），然后签上你的英语姓名就行了。而要更有诚意，你需要选择使用下列的范例：

♪ MP3 03-12

单词补充　♪ MP3 03-13
- ★ **joyous** ['dʒɔɪəs] a 喜悦的
- **abundance** [ə'bʌndəns] n 丰富
- **joyful** ['dʒɔɪfəl] a 欢欣的
- ★ **meaningful** ['minɪŋfəl] a 有意义的
- ★ **opportunity** [,ɑpɚ'tjunətɪ] n 机会
- ★ **success** [sək'sɛs] n 成功

At this joyous* time of year, we are grateful for your support. We wish you abundance*, happiness, and peace in a new year. Happy holidays!

　　在今年欢乐的时刻，我们很感谢您的支持。祝您在新的一年丰收、幸福与平安！佳节愉快！

We wish you and your family a joyful* holiday season.

　　我们祝福您和您的家人，佳节愉快。

Thank you for working with us this year. We would like to wish you a happy and meaningful* year.

　　谢谢您今年与我们的合作。祝您有个快乐与有意义的一年。

On this special day, we would like to thank you for giving us the opportunity* to serve you. Merry Christmas! We wish you much success* in the new year.

　　在这个特殊的日子，我们要谢谢您让我们有机会为您服务。圣诞快乐！祝您未来一年更成功。

Lesson 4
席卷全球的运动热潮!

学习重点1	通过体育新闻,仿写文章
学习重点2	看懂短篇体育新闻
学习重点3	和人讨论喜欢的球队与球星
学习重点4	简短介绍喜欢的运动

Unit 1 用英语认识运动

休闲运动越来越受到人们的重视与喜爱，通过以下阅读，我们来学习与运动有关的单词与语法。

♪ MP3 04-01

Sports* play an important role❶ in many countries and cultures. There are four major professional sports leagues in the United States: Major League Baseball (MLB), the National Basketball Association (NBA), the National Football League (NFL), and the National Hockey League (NHL). Games* played by these four major leagues are watched* and supported* by their fans* around the world. These four leagues have teams representing different cities❷. There are also minor leagues*. In the US, high schools and universities also have organized sports teams. Games played by students are also very popular*.

运动在许多国家与文化中扮演着重要的角色。美国有四个职业运动联盟：美国职业棒球大联盟（MLB）、美国职业篮球联盟（NBA）、美国国家橄榄球联盟（NFL）和美国国家冰球联盟（NHL）。这四个职业运动联盟的比赛在全世界各地都有球迷观看与支持。四个联盟都有代表不同城市的球队。有些也有小联盟。在美国，中学和大学也有自己的球队。学生球队的比赛也很受欢迎。

实用句型

❶ _____ play an important role
   _____ 扮演重要的角色

❷ _____ represent _____ city
   代表 _____ 城市

单词补充 ♪ MP3 04-02
- ★ sports [spɔrts] n 运动
- ★ game [gem] n 比赛
- ★ watch [watʃ] v 看球赛
- ★ support [səˈpɔrt] v 支持
- ★ fan [fæn] n 球迷
- ★ minor league ph 小联盟
- ★ popular [ˈpɑpjələr] a 受欢迎的

▶ 再来用刚刚学过的单词与句型造几个句子。

Major and minor league teams are often run by different owners.
大联盟与小联盟球队常由不同的拥有者来经营。

This game was watched by an audience of 20 million.
这场球赛观看的观众有 2 000 万人。

The news said about three quarters of American adults are sports fans.
新闻说四分之三的美国成年人都是运动迷。

That policy is supported by them.
这项政策受到他们的支持。

Korean dramas and music are very popular now.
现在韩国戏剧与音乐很受欢迎。

Lesson 4

MLB the Major League Baseball 美国职业棒球大联盟

NBA the National Basketball Association 美国职业篮球联盟

NFL the National Football League 美国国家橄榄球联盟

NHL the National Hockey League 美国国家冰球联盟

美国四大职业运动联盟 (four professional sports leagues)

语法教室

❶ 表示有没有的 there is 和 there are

There is + 单数名词
- 肯定：**There is a sandwich** on the plate.
  盘子上有一块三明治。
- 疑问：**Is there** a sandwich on the plate?
  盘子上有没有一块三明治？

There are + 复数名词
- 肯定：**There are sandwiches** on the plate.
  盘子上有很多块三明治。
- 疑问：**Are there** sandwiches on the plate?
  盘子上有没有很多块三明治？

❷ 动词主被动

可观察下列两组例句，学习动词主被动时句子意思的小小不同之处。基本上，当使用动词主动时，主语通常为人；使用动词被动时，主语通常为事物或被施予动作的人。

- Two players can **play** this online game.（主动）
  两个人可以玩这个线上游戏。
- This online game can **be played** by two players.（被动）
  这个线上游戏可以两个人玩。

- Who **broke** the window?（主动）
  谁打破了那扇窗户？
- The window **was broken**.（被动）
  那扇窗户被打破了。

❸ 冒号（：）的使用

说明或解释

This is their travel plan: going to Australia. 这是他们的旅游计划：去澳洲。

列出一系列的名单

There are **four major professional sports leagues** in the United States: **the Major League Baseball (MLB), the National Basketball Association (NBA), the National Football League (NFL), and the National Hockey League (NHL).**
美国有四个职业运动联盟：美国职业棒球大联盟（MLB）、美国职业篮球联盟（NBA）、美国国家橄榄球联盟（NFL）和美国国家冰球联盟（NHL）。

引述谈话内容

She said: "This is a new era." 她说："这是个新世代。"

表示副标题

Foreigners Shot Dead in Burkina Faso: A Terrorist Attack
外国人在布基纳法索遭枪杀：恐怖袭击事件。

> 了解完美国的职业运动，我们当然也得来一篇和职业运动相关的英语写作。就利用上面学过的单词、语法和句型。

我们先来看一篇有关职业棒球联盟（**Professional Baseball League**）及篮球联赛（**League Basketball**）的文章。经过套用与改写后，我们就有了以下的文章：

Sports play an important role in JanPan. There are two major popular professional sports leagues in JanPan: Central League Baseball and BJ League Basketball. Games played by these two major leagues are watched and supported by their fans around the country. These two leagues have teams representing different companies. High schools and universities in Japan also have organized their baseball or basketball teams. Games played by students are also very popular.

运动在日本扮演着重要的角色。在日本有两个比较受欢迎的职业运动联盟：中央棒球联盟和BJ超级篮球联赛（SBL）。全日本的球迷观看并支持这两个联盟的球赛。这两个联盟的球队代表不同的公司。在日本，高中及大学也都有自己的棒球队或篮球队。由学生出赛的球赛也很受欢迎。

▶ 虽然仍有许多模糊处需要进一步定义，但是 **professional**（职业）跟 **amateur**（业余）的差别在于运动员是否利用该项运动来谋生。

Unit 2 谈论热门队伍与球星

对于旅外的选手，支持者总是非常注意他们的动向，并给予支持，如果想要最先得知该选手状况的话，看英语报道是最直接的方式，接下来练习看与运动相关的报道。利用媒体新闻来学习单词与句型，然后来看如何用英语谈论运动及你喜爱的队伍与球星。

♪ MP3 04-04

Wei-Yin Chen(陈伟殷), the left-handed * free agent * starter, has agreed to sign with * the Miami Marlins at $16 million per year for the first five years plus a sixth-year vesting option. He and the famous Japanese left fielder, Ichiro Suzuki, now are teammates *.

Chen's deal reportedly * is the richest contract ever given. That deal is worth * more than the signing between the New York Yankees of Major League Baseball (MLB) with another Taidong * pitcher *, Chien-Ming Wang (王建民), at the amount of a one-year deal of US$5 million.

据报道，左投左打的陈伟殷已经同意与迈阿密马林鱼签下前五年每年价值 1 600 万美元，外带第 6 年 1 600 万选择权的合约。陈伟殷与来自日本的知名的左外野手铃木一郎目前是同队战友。
这张合约是马林鱼给予投手的最大合约。该合约的价值高于 2009 年另一位来自台东县的投手王建民与美国职业棒球大联盟 (MLB) 纽约洋基队所签订的每年美金 500 万合约。

语法教室

Give 的用法

给 give

My friend **gave me a dog**.
= My friend **gave a dog to me**. 我朋友给我一只狗。

离开 give away

It is difficult to **give a dog away**. 要把狗送走很难。

帮忙 give a hand

She asked me to **give her a hand**. 她要我帮她忙。

还 give back

My mother asked me to **give it back**. 我妈要我把它送回去。

放弃 give up

I will not **give up** the dog. 我不会放弃这只狗。

单词补充 ♪ MP3 04-05

* left-handed ['lɛft'hændɪd] a. 左撇子的、惯用左手的
* free agent ph. 自由球员
* sign with... ph. ……与……签订合约
* teammate ['tim,met] n. 队友
* reportedly [rɪ'portɪdlɪ] ad. 据报道
* ...is worth ph. 价值……
* pitcher ['pɪtʃɚ] n. 投手

Unit 3 火红球队和球星名单

谈论运动，尤其是棒球，一定得提及火红球队与球星，哪些球队跟球员是我们一定得知道的呢？依据 MLB 网站 (http://mlb.mlb.com/home)，各球队信息如下：

MLB Teams 联盟球队

American League 美国联盟

Baltimore Orioles 巴尔的摩金莺队
Boston Red Sox 波士顿红袜队
Chicago White Sox 芝加哥白袜队
Cleveland Indians 克里夫兰印第安人队
Detroit Tigers 底特律老虎队
Huston Astros 休士顿太空人队
Kansas City Royals 堪萨斯市皇家队
Los Angeles Angels 洛杉矶天使队
Minnesota Twins 明尼苏达双城队
New York Yankees 纽约洋基队
Oakland Athletics 奥克兰运动家队
Seattle Mariners 德州游骑兵队
Tampa Bay Rays 坦帕湾光芒队
Texas Rangers 西雅图水手队
Toronto Blue Jays 多伦多蓝鸟队

National League 国家联盟

Arizona Diamondbacks 亚利桑那响尾蛇队
Atlanta Braves 亚特兰大勇士队
Chicago Cubs 芝加哥小熊队
Cincinnati Reds 辛辛那提红人队
Colorado Rockies 科罗拉多洛矶队
Los Angeles Dodgers 洛杉矶道奇队
Miami Marlins 迈阿密马林鱼队
Milwaukee Brewers 密尔瓦基酿酒人队
New York Mets 纽约大都会队
Philadelphia Phillies 费城费城人队
Pittsburgh Pirates 匹兹堡海盗队
San Diego Padres 圣地亚哥教士队
San Francisco Giants 旧金山巨人队
St. Louis Cardinals 圣路易红雀队
Washington Nationals 华盛顿国民队

▶ 你并不需要熟记上述球队队名，可以看球赛时慢慢来记，也可以多了解你谈话对象的城市球队，这样一来，要与美国人用英语谈论棒球运动就有个好开始。

现在来看看 Business Insider 排名的目前最活跃的五十位运动员中，前八名最活跃的运动员及他们所代表的运动吧。

Ronda Rousey 龙达·鲁西	USC Fighter 格斗选手	Mixed Martial Arts 综合格斗
LeBron James 勒布朗·詹姆斯	Forward, Cleveland Cavaliers 克里夫兰骑士队前锋	basketball 篮球
Serena Williams 小威廉姆斯	Tennis Player 网球员	tennis 网球
Cristiano Ronaldo C·罗纳尔多	Forward, Real Madrid 皇家马德里足球俱乐部前锋	soccer 足球
Usain Bolt 尤塞恩·博尔特	Sprinter 短跑选手	sprint 短跑
Simone Biles 西蒙娜·拜尔斯	Gymnast 体操选手	gymnastics 体操
Lionel Messi 莱昂内尔·梅西	Forward, FC Barcelona FC 巴塞罗那队前锋	soccer 足球
Clayton Kershaw 克莱顿·柯萧	Pitcher, Los Angels Dodgers 洛杉矶道奇队投手	baseball 棒球

实用会话

 MP3 04-06

问题句型 / 回答

What's your favorite team?
你喜欢的球队是哪一队？
→ My favorite NBA team is the Los Angeles Lakers.
我喜欢的 NBA 球队是洛杉矶湖人队。

Who's your favorite player?
你喜欢的球员是哪一位？
→ Serena Williams is definitely my favorite tennis player.
我最喜欢的网球运动员绝对是小威廉姆斯。

How did the player perform in the competition?
那位选手在比赛中表现如何？
→ Lionel Messi's performance in the game won him the European Golden Shoe Award.
梅西在比赛中的表现让他赢得欧洲金靴奖。

How did that player inspire you?
那位选手如何激励了你？
→ I was inspired by the player when he said "We have to believe in each other."
那位球员说"我们必须互相信任"时激励了我。

What was the result of the conest? 比赛的结果如何？
→ The young gymnast received a perfect ten. 那位年轻的体操选手获得了满分十分。

Which team is the winner?
优胜队伍是哪个队？
→ Beating the Yankee, 6-5, the Boston Red Sox made itself a winning team.
波士顿红袜队以 6:5 击败洋基队，成为优胜队伍。

对话情境 ♪ MP3 04-07

Ⓐ: Do you like sports?

Ⓑ: Yes, I am a fan of sports.

Ⓐ: Do you play any sports?

Ⓑ: Yes, I go swimming in the morning every day. I used to play basketball and do judo*, too.

Ⓐ: Swimming! That's my favorite sport, too.

Ⓑ: Did you watch the swimming competition* on TV yesterday?

Ⓐ: I did. Ledecky and her teammates won gold in the 4×200-meter freestyle* relay*.

Ⓑ: That's amazing. Although she is young, she has already set several world records.

Ⓐ: Yes, can you believe she started swimming only at the age of six?

Ⓑ: I am more inspired by her spirit*, and she said, "I just like to swim fast, I don't think about the distance*."

A：你喜欢运动吗？

B：是的，我是个运动迷。

A：你做什么运动吗？

B：是的，我每天早晨都游泳，以前也会打篮球和练柔道。

A：游泳！那也是我最喜欢的运动。

B：你昨天有没有看电视上的游泳比赛？

A：有啊！莱德克伊和她的队友在 4×200 米自由式接力中赢得了金牌。

B：太惊人了！虽然她很年轻，但是她已经缔造了多项世界纪录。

A：是的，你能相信她 6 岁就开始游泳吗？

B：她的精神更是激励了我，她说："我只是想游快一点，而不会去思考距离有多远。"

语法教室

单词补充 ♪ MP3 04-08

★ judo ['dʒudo] n. 柔道
★ competition [ˌkɑmpə'tɪʃən] n. 比赛
★ freestyle ['fri,staɪl] n.（游泳）自由式的
★ relay [rɪ'le] n. 接力
★ spirit ['spɪrɪt] n. 精神
★ distance ['dɪstəns] n. 距离

go、play、do，到底使用哪一个动词来谈论运动呢？看起来很复杂，其实很简单，只要辨别运动的类型就可以了。

使用 "-ing" 结尾的运动使用 "go"
例如：**go swimming**（游泳）、**go hiking**（徒步旅行）

体能类运动使用 "do"
例如：**do judo**（练柔道）、**do aerobics**（做有氧舞蹈）

球类运动使用 "play"
例如：**play soccer**（踢足球）、**play table tennis**（打桌球）

◆ used to 与 be used to 的小专栏 ◆

问题：如何使用 used to 与 be used to 来表示习惯呢？

used to（曾经） + **动词原形** → 表示**以前的习惯**

I **used to** go to bed after midnight.
我以前都在午夜后才睡觉。
He **used to** drink a lot.
他以前都喝很多。

这些都是过去的经验，现在我都很早睡，他知道喝酒应适量。

be used to + **动词 ing** → 表示**养成习惯**

肯定用法

I **am used to** going to bed before midnight.
我已经习惯在午夜前上床睡觉。
He **is used to** drinking properly.
他已经习惯饮酒要适量。

否定用法

I **did not** use to go to bed before midnight.
我以前都不会在午夜前上床睡觉。
He **used not to** smoke.
他以前不抽烟。

疑问句

Did you use to go to bed after midnight?
你以前都在午夜过后才上床睡觉吗？（过去的经验）
Is he used to going biking on weekends?
他是否周末都习惯去骑自行车？（现在的习惯）

Unit 4 属于四季的休闲运动

四季分别为 spring（春）、summer（夏）、autumn / fall（秋）及 winter（冬），适合各个季节从事的运动有哪些？

春季 Spring

适合春天的运动　　　　　　　　　　　　　　　MP3 04-09

Golf is a sport for spring. Clubs are used to hit a ball* into each hole* on the golf course*. Players with the lowest number of strokes* are winners. Playing golf is healthy, exciting, and fun. You can go outdoors and play with your family. More people are learning to play golf. Tiger Woods inspired children of all ages to start playing golf.

单词补充　MP3 04-10
* hit a ball ph 击球
* hole [hol] n 球洞
* golf course ph 球场
* stroke [strok] n 杆

打高尔夫球属于春天的运动。打高尔夫球使用球棍将球打入球场上的洞内。杆数最低的球员是优胜者。打高尔夫球很健康、令人振奋及有趣。你可以到户外与家人一起打高尔夫球。现在有更多的人在学打高尔夫球。老虎伍兹激励了各个年龄层的孩子开始打高尔夫球。

▶ 打高尔夫球不只是运动，它同时也是身份与地位的象征。我们来认识一下与高尔夫球相关的基本常识与其他用语。

❶ **Golf**（高尔夫球）代表四个英语字母：**Green**（自然）、**Oxygen**（氧气）、**Light**（阳光）和 **Friendship**（友谊）。

❷ **albatross**（信天翁）为低于标准杆三杆，也称为"双鹰（**double eagle**）"。**eagle**（老鹰）为低于标准杆二杆。**bogey** 为"高于标准杆一杆"。高于二杆为 **double bogey**；高于三杆称 **triple bogey**，以此类推。

❸ **handicap**（差点或差杆），指球员打球实际总杆与球场标准杆之间的相差杆数。**hole-in-one** 为"一杆进洞"。**par** 为"标准杆数"。

夏季 Summer

适合夏天的运动就是直排轮了　　　　　　　　　MP3 04-11

Rollerblading is a sport for summer. It is terrific and fun. You can go rollerblading* almost anytime and anywhere including walking paths*, parks, courts*, bike paths, and private driveways. Rollerblading racing is very competitive. It is a sport for people of all ages. The best thing about rollerblading is you can go alone or with friends and family.

单词补充　MP3 04-12
* go rollerblading ph 滑轮滑
* walking path ph 步道
* court [kort] n 球场

轮滑属于夏天的运动，很棒又有趣。你几乎可以随时随地轮滑，包括步道、公园、球场、自行车道与私人车道。轮滑比赛很具竞争性。它是适合所有年龄层的运动。轮滑最棒的地方是你可以自己滑或和朋友与家人一起滑。

秋季 Autumn / fall

近来全民热衷露营，朋友圈刷屏的也是周末的露营活动，camping 露营在天气宜人的秋季再适合不过。

🎵 MP3 04-13

Autumn is the ideal season for camping. Hot summer days are behind us. Cool air* and warm food* is the perfect match* for campers* in autumn. Falling tree leaves* also help you to improve your photograph skills*; the perfect weather for hiking relaxes* your mind and body. There are many reasons for you to go camping in autumn. What is your favorite reason?

秋天是露营的最理想季节。我们已经摆脱了炎热的夏季。对露营的朋友来说，凉爽的空气与热食是秋天最完美的组合。落叶也能帮你改善摄影技巧；适合健步走的完美天气让你的身心放松。秋天去露营的原因有许多。你最喜欢的原因是什么？

实用单词 🎵 MP3 04-14

- outdoor recreational activity ph 户外休闲活动
- natural environment ph 自然环境
- picnic ['pɪknɪk] n 野餐
- tent [tɛnt] n 帐篷
- scouting ['skaʊtɪŋ] n 侦查
- fishing ['fɪʃɪŋ] n 捕鱼
- climbing ['klaɪmɪŋ] n 爬山

单词补充 🎵 MP3 04-15

★ go camping ph 去露营
★ cool air ph 凉爽的空气
★ warm food ph 热食
★ the perfect match ph 完美搭配
★ camper ['kæmpɚ] n 露营者
★ falling tree leaves ph 落叶
★ photograph skills ph 摄影技巧
★ relax [rɪ'læks] v 放松

接下来，就利用刚刚学到的这些单词来写篇小短文吧！

🎵 MP3 04-16

Camping is an outdoor recreational activity. Campers have the chance to get away from cities and have contact with the natural environment. Camping is different from a one-day trip or picnicking. Campers at least stay outdoors one night. Campers build their tents for scouting. Some of them will also go fishing and climbing.

露营是户外的休闲活动。露营者有机会远离城市，接近自然环境。露营与一天的旅行或野餐不同。露友至少会在户外过一夜。露营者搭盖自己的帐篷来侦查。有些人也会去捕鱼和爬山。

冬季 Winter

冷飕飕的冬天,确实不是进行户外运动的好季节,但是如果要动,又要应景,那么首推滑雪了。

♪ MP3 04-17

Ski resorts * often start to operate * in the middle December, so skiing is the best sport for winter. If you have never had the opportunity to ski, you have missed out on a lot of fun. With instruction *, everyone can learn how to ski easily *. It is believed the best time to learn how to ski should be at a young age. Ski resorts have provided * classes for families and children of all skill levels. They also offer services including equipment rental * and food.

滑雪场通常都在12月中营运,滑雪也是最适合冬天的运动,如果你未曾滑过雪,你就错失了许多乐趣。经过教授,每个人都可以轻松学会滑雪。学习滑雪最好尽早开始。滑雪场会提供不同程度的课程给家庭和小孩。他们也提供包括设备租用和饮食等服务。

语法教室

表示"包括" including、included、inclusive 的用法

The studio **including** utilities is for rent.
= The studio, utilities **included**, is for rent.
= The studio is for rent, utilities **inclusive**.
= 这个套房要出租,包水电。

单词补充 ♪ MP3 04-18

* **ski resort** pn 滑雪场
* **operate** [ˈɑpəret] v 营运、运作
* **instruction** [ɪnˈstrʌkʃən] n 教导
* **easily** [ˈizɪlɪ] adv 轻易地
* **provide** [prəˈvaɪd] v 提供
* **equipment rental** pn 设备租用

利用我们学过的运动以及相关用语和语法,你也可以用英语写一篇在你喜欢的季节中可以从事的运动!更可以用英语聊聊最新的赛事与你的偶像运动选手的优异表现!

Unit 1 奥林匹克运动会

在 **Lesson 4**，我们谈的都是运动，而在 **Lesson 5**，我们将学习如何用英语来讨论大型的运动赛事，像奥运会、世界杯等，这些也是与人用英语来谈论运动的好题材！通过阅读下列英语短文，我们先来了解奥运会的起源。

The first ancient Olympic Games can be traced back to 776 B.C., and the games continued for nearly 12 centuries. The Games were celebrated every four years. But in 393 A.D. the Games were banned. The ancient Olympic Games were held in Olympia, the island of "Peoples." The ancient Olympic Games were closely linked to the religious festivals of Zeus to show the performance of young people and to promote good relation ships among cities of Greece.

第一届古代奥林匹克运动会可以追溯至公元前 776 年，比赛一直持续举办了近 12 个世纪，每四年举办一次，但是在 393 年，比赛被禁止了。古代的奥林匹克运动会在"人类之岛"奥林匹亚举行。古代的奥林匹克运动会与宙斯的祭典有密切关系，用来展现年轻人的表现及促进希腊城市之间的良好关系。

实用单词 🎵 MP3 05-01

trace back ph 追溯至	The early history of this concept can be **traced back** to India. 这个概念的最早历史可以追溯至印度。
continue for ph 持续	The bike path in the downtown area **continues for** several kilometers. 市区的自行车道延绵了数公里。
ban [bæn] v 禁止	Chewing gum is **banned** in Singapore. 新加坡禁止吃口香糖。
link to ph 连接	The development of tourism is closely **linked to** the building of infrastructure. 旅游业的发展与基础建设的建立有密切关系。
promote good relationships between... 推广与……之间的良好关系	This policy aims to **promote good relationships between** managers and employees. 这个政策的目标是为了促进劳资之间的良好关系。

Lesson 5

对话情境 🎵 MP3 05-02

A: Do you know how long the history of the Olympic Games is?

B: According to history, the ancient Olympic Games can be traced to 776 B.C..

A: Wow! That's long.

A：你知道奥运会的历史有多久吗？

B：根据历史记载，可以追溯至公元前776年。

A：哇！好悠久。

成为奥运会选手是每位运动员的最大梦想与成就，下列文章告诉我们如何成为奥运会选手？

Athletes required long years of training to take part in* the Olympic Games. In addition*, they must first comply with rules in the Olympic Charter* and the International Federation* (IF) of their sport. The National Olympic Committee* (NOC) of the athlete's country will then enter their athletes into the Games.

运动员需要多年训练才能参与奥运会。除此之外，他们必须遵守《奥林匹克宪章》与所属运动国际组织的规定。运动员所在国的国家奥委会会为运动员报名参加奥运。

单词补充 🎵 MP3 05-03
- ★ take part in ph 参与
- ★ in addition ph 除此之外
- ★ The Olympic Charter ph 《奥林匹克宪章》
- ★ International Federation ph 国际总会
- ★ The National Olympic Committee ph 国家奥运委员会

语法教室

除了，包含……

in addition,
besides,
on the top of that,
} + 主语 + 动词

In addition, we will stop in Hong Kong on our way to Australia.
Besides, we will stop in Hong Kong on our way to Australia.
On the top of that, we will stop in Hong Kong on our way to Australia.
除此之外，我在去澳洲的途中会停留在香港。

除了，不包含……

except for + 名词,
apart from + 名词, + 主语 + 动词
aside from + 名词,

Except for Australia, we will visit all Oceanian countries.
Apart from Australia, we will visit all Oceanian countries.
Aside from Australia, we will visit all Oceanian countries.
除了澳洲之外，我们会去大洋洲所有的国家。

对话情境 ♪ MP3 05-04

A: I'm thinking of taking part in the Olympic Games.

B: You? As an athlete?

A: Yes, as an athlete.

B: What's your sport and how many years have you been trained?

A: I have been playing golf for many years.

B: Yes, golf will be played at the 2020 Summer Olympics.

A：我想参加奥运会。

B：你？以运动员身份？

A：是的，以运动员身份。

B：你要参加的运动是什么，你接受了多少年的训练？

A：我打高尔夫球很多年了。

B：是的，高尔夫球将会是 2020 年夏季奥运会的比赛项目。

▶ 接下来，我们以跆拳道这个奥运会比赛项目为例，来看获奖情形。

Taekwondo* is one of sports at the Summer Olympic Games *. It was a demonstration sport * before 2000. Male and female athletes compete in different groups of body weight. Chi Shu-ju is the youngest athlete to win a medal * at the age of 17, and Hadi Saei from Iran is the oldest at the age of 32. A total of 40 gold medals *, 40 silver medals * and 64 bronze medals * have been awarded since 2000.

跆拳道是夏季奥运会的竞赛项目之一。在 2000 年之前，跆拳道是奥运会的示范赛项目。男性和女性运动员在不同的体重组别中比赛。奥运会跆拳道奖牌得主得奖时年纪最轻的是纪淑如，为 17 岁，伊朗的哈迪萨依赢得奖牌时的年龄最大，为 32 岁。自 2000 年以来，所颁出的奖牌共 40 金、40 银及 64 铜。

单词补充 ♪ MP3 05-05

* **taekwondo** [taɪˈkɒndo] n 跆拳道
* **Summer Olympic Games** ph 夏季奥运会
* **demonstration sport** ph 示范赛项目
* **medal** [ˈmɛdl] n 奖牌
* **gold medal** ph 金牌
* **silver medal** ph 银牌
* **bronze medal** ph 铜牌

Unit 2 国际足联世界杯

The FIFA World Cup is a quadrennial world championship for men's national football teams organized by FIFA since 1930. The numbers of active football players are about 200 million around the world. As of mid-2007, FIFA has 208 member associations. Football presents huge market potential in Asia and North America.

国际足联世界杯是由国际足联自 1930 年以来所主办的每四年一次由国家男子足球队所参赛的世界锦标赛。全世界有约 2 亿活跃球员。截至 2007 年中，FIFA 的会员协会已经增加至 208 个。足球具有极大的市场潜能，特别是在亚洲与北美。

实用单词

♪ MP3 05-06

quadrennial [kwɒdˈrenɪəl]
a 每四年的
The FIFA World Cup is a quadrennial sporting event.
FIFA 世界杯是四年一度的运动赛事。

men's national football teams
ph 男子足球国家队
The report introduced players in the men's national football team.
报道介绍男子足球国家队的选手。

decade [ˈdɛked] n 十年
Time has changed and things now are not what they were a decade ago.
时间已经改变了，事情不再是十年前的样子。

the leading global sport
ph 全球主要运动
Football is considered the leading global sport since it is one of the top ten sports in all countries measured.
足球被视为主要的全球运动，因为它是所有调查国家中的十大运动之一。

active football player
ph 活跃足球员
Leionel Messi has been voted as the most popular active football player in the world.
梅西被票选为全世界最受欢迎的活跃足球员。

market potential
ph 市场潜能
Market potential estimates maximum total sales revenue of a product during a certain period of time.
市场潜力评估一个产品在特定时间的最大总营销收入。

对话情境　♪MP3 05-07

A: Have you ever watched any game of the FIFA World Cup?

B: Of course. I am a big fan of football. It's a big quadrennial event to me.

A: Who do you think is the most popular active football player in the world?

B: Out of 200 million players, I like Leionel Messi the best. I am even planning to go to the FIFA World Cup in 2022.

A: You must be kidding me.

A: 你看过任何 FIFA 世界杯足球赛吗？

B: 当然，我可是个足球迷。对我来说可是四年一度的大盛事。

A: 你认为谁是全世界最受欢迎的活跃足球运动员？

B: 在 2 亿球员中，我最喜欢梅西了。我还在计划 2022 年要去看世界杯足球赛。

A: 你不是认真的吧！

> **注意** 你在开玩笑吧？／你不是认真的吧！
> Are you kidding? = Are you kidding me?
> = You must be kidding. = You must be kidding me.
> 用在听到很难以相信情况的说明之后。

听完对话之后，接下来看看 2014 年世界杯足球赛的盛况。

On July 24, 2014, the 2014 FIFA World Cup Final* took place in Rio de Janeiro, Brazil. In extra time*, Germany defeated Argentina 1-0 scored. Before the match*, Germany and Argentina had reached World Cup Final respectively* seven times and four times. This was the first World Cup title* of Germany since its reunification.

The FIFA World Cup is the most widely viewed sporting event* in the world with an estimated 715.1 million people watching the final match*, a ninth of the entire world population*. FIFA executives were accused of* taking bribes* totaling* more than $150 million in the 2015 FIFA scandal.

单词补充　♪MP3 05-08

* **The FIFA World Cup Final** n 世界杯足球赛决赛
* **extra time** n 延长赛
* **...scored by** ph 由……得分
* **match** [mætʃ] n 比赛
* **respectively** [rɪˈspɛktɪvlɪ] adv 个别地
* **World Cup title** n 世界杯冠军
* **the most widely viewed sporting event** ph 最多人观看赛事
* **the final match** ph 决赛
* **entire world population** ph 世界总人口
* **scandal** [ˈskændl] n 丑闻
* **be accused of** ph 被控诉
* **take bribes** ph 收取贿赂
* **total** [ˈtotl] v 总共 a 总计的

在 2014 年 7 月 24 日，2014 FIFA 世界杯足球赛决赛在巴西里约热内卢开打。在加时赛中，德国以 1：0 击败阿根廷。在这场比赛之前，德国与阿根廷分别进入决赛七次与四次。这是德国自东西德合并后第一次赢得世界杯足球赛冠军。

世界杯是观看人数最多的运动赛事，估计有约 7.151 亿人观看决赛，约是全世界人口的九分之一。在 2015 年的 FIFA 丑闻中，FIFA 执行官员被控诉收取贿赂金额高达 1.5 亿美元。

学会了单词，更要能够活用，接下来就来看看用刚刚学过的单词造的例句吧！

- **The FIFA World Cup Final** attracted a big audience.
  FIFA 世界杯足球赛决赛吸引了大批观众。
- The 2016 Summer Olympics was held in **Rio de Janeiro, Brazil** on Aug 5-21.
  2016 年夏季奥运会于 8 月 5—21 日在巴西里约热内卢举行。
- According to statistics, most team won during **extra time**.
  根据统计，大部分的球队都在加时赛中获胜。
- In eight **matches**, six goals were **scored by** him.
  在八场比赛中，他得了六分。
- FIFA announced that the 2026 World Cup will be held in the United States, Mexico and Canada respectively.
  国际足联宣布 2026 年世界杯将分别在美国、墨西哥和加拿大举行。
- Germany held four **World Cup titles**, and so did Italy.
  德国与意大利皆赢过四次世界杯足球赛冠军。
- Football, not the Olympic Games, is **the most widely viewed sporting event**.
  观看人数最多的运动赛事是足球而不是奥运会。
- The **estimated** number of audience was about 1,000.
  估算的观众数目约为 1 000 人。
- About a ninth of **entire world population** watched **the final match**.
  世界上九分之一的人口观看决赛。
- The **scandal** involved briberies and money laundering.
  丑闻涉及贿赂与洗钱。
- He was **accused of** stealing.
  他被控偷窃。
- The mayor was caught **taking briberies**.
  市长被控收受贿赂。
- How much in **total** will that house cost you?
  房子总共多少钱？

▶ 特别注意副词 "respectively（分别地）" 这个单词，来看更多的相关造句吧！

- We'll visit our friends in Sydney and Brisbane **respectively**.
  我们会分别拜访在悉尼及布里斯班的朋友。
- You need to understand the meanings on this page **respectively**.
  你必须分别了解本页中的意思。
- The prices of petroleum and natural gas will **respectively** decrease by 3% and 2% next week.
  下周石油与天然气价格将分别调降 3% 及 2%。

对话情境

🎵 MP3 05-09

A: Do you know what the most widely viewed sporting event is?

B: Let me guess. The Olympic Games?

A: Wrong! Let me tell you it's FIFA World Cup.

B: I am not surprised.

A: Yeah, did you watch the final match of Germany and Argentina?

B: I missed the game.

A: What? You didn't see the goal scored by Mario Götze in extra time. You surely missed the most exciting game in history.

B: You are telling me.

A：你知道观看人数最多的运动赛事是什么吗？

B：让我猜猜。奥运会？

A：错！我跟你说是 FIFA 世界杯足球赛。

B：我一点也不惊讶。

A：对啊，你看了德国对阿根廷的决赛吗？

B：我没看到。

A：什么？你没看到马里奥·格策在加时赛中得到的那一分。你真的错过史上最精彩的球赛了。

B：没错。

NOTICE!

Tell 的惯用语用法

You are **telling** me.
Tell me about it.
你说得没错。

Tell me another.
我可不相信。

I am **telling** you.
这很重要。

Don't **tell** me you don't know.
你不会不知道吧。

Don't let him **tell** you that.
别相信他。

与足球相关的重要英语用语

dribbling 盘球过人
fouls 犯规
free kick 任意球
goal area 禁区
goal kick 球门球
Handball 手球
sliding tackling 铲球
Wall of Players 人墙
Red Card 红牌出场
Yellow Card 黄牌警告
Own Goal 乌龙球
Stoppage time / Injury time / Loss time 伤停时间
tackling / intercepting 截球

Penalty Mark 点球罚球点
passing 传球
penalty kick 罚球
shot 射门
Kick-Off 开球
offside 越位

马拉松

我们先来看几项与马拉松有关的事实：

The modern Athens Marathon commemorates the messenger of Soldier Pheidippides; he collapsed and died after delivering the victory message.
现代的雅典马拉松是为了纪念信使士兵菲迪皮德斯；他在传达战胜信息后倒地死亡。

The official distance of marathon is 42.195 kilometers.
全马的距离为 42.195 公里。

In 2013, Running USA reported approximately 550,637 marathon finishers in the United States.
据美国路跑协会报告，在 2013 年，完成马拉松的跑者达 550 637 人。

实用单词

♪ MP3 05-10

marathon ['mærəˌθɑn] n 马拉松	A lot of people believe that the key to successful **marathon** training is to start right. 许多人认为成功的马拉松训练为正确的开始。
messenger ['mɛsndʒɚ] n 信使	In the ancient time, people used doves as the **messenger**. 在古时候，人们使用鸽子当信使。
commemorate [kə'mɛməˌret] v 纪念	On the Dragon Boat Festival, we **commemorate** the patriotic poet, Qu Yuan. 端午节时，我们纪念爱国诗人屈原。
collapse [kə'læps] v 倒塌	Due to earthquake, many buildings **collapsed**. 因为地震，许多建筑物倒塌了。
original [ə'rɪdʒənl] a 原始的	Customers are familiar with the story behind the **original** design. 顾客很熟悉原始设计背后的故事。
course [kors] n 跑道	This **course** map clearly shows you the starting and finishing point of the marathon running. 这张跑道图清楚地显示了马拉松赛的起点与终点。

语法教室

legend has it that 主语 + 动词过去式（传说）

Legend has it that a cow kicked over a lantern in a barn and started the Chicago Fire of 1871.
传说一头牛踢翻了谷仓中的油灯并且引发 1871 年的芝加哥大火。

Legend has it that she became a fish. 传说她变成鱼。

对话情境

🎵 MP3 05-11

A: What do you know about marathon running?

B: I know the story of Pheidippides. It's a big achievement* for many runners.

A: It requires gradual* training because the distance of a full marathon is 42.195 kilometers.

B: 42.195 kilometers? It's about a 30-minute drive.

A: It is no easy task*. At the beginning, you may need to run about 5 kilometers.

B: I wonder what people are thinking of when they are running marathons.

A: That's a good question. According to a study, most runners spend their time thinking about pace* and distance.

B: Do runners complain discomfort* when running?

A: They should not be feeling pain. If they do, they should stop immediately.

B: You sound like an expert*. Why don't you run in a marathon?

A: Well, I need to find more free time.

A：你对跑马拉松了解多少？

B：我知道菲迪皮德斯的故事。对许多跑者而言，跑马拉松是个大成就。

A：它必须循序渐进地训练，因为全程马拉松的距离为 42.195 公里。

B：42.195 公里？开车约要 30 分钟。

A：不容易，开始时，你可能需要跑 5 公里。

B：我在想跑马拉松的时候，跑者在想些什么？

A：好问题。一份研究指出大部分的跑者都把时间花在思考速度和距离上。

B：跑者在跑步时会抱怨不舒服吗？

A：在当时，他们应该没有感觉到疼痛。如果有不舒服，应该马上停止。

B：你听起来像个专家。你为什么不跑马拉松呢？

A：我需找出更多闲暇时间。

▶ 在这两个有关运动的单元中，我们学习了个人喜爱及大型的运动赛事，从历史渊源到最近的发展，我们学习专门的英语词汇与用法。再学习一些运动规则与更多的专有名词，认识与熟悉它们，你就绝对是个运动通，用英语谈运动，轻轻松松！

单词补充 🎵 MP3 05-12

★ **achievement** [əˈtʃɪvmənt] n 成就
★ **gradual** [ˈɡrædʒuəl] a 逐渐的
★ **task** [tæsk] n 任务
★ **pace** [pes] n 步伐
★ **discomfort** [dɪsˈkʌmfət] n 不舒服
★ **expert** [ˈɛkspɚt] n 专家 a 专家的

Lesson 6

不可不知的电影二三事!

学习重点 1 | 约外国朋友看电影

学习重点 2 | 用英语和朋友讨论喜欢的电影

学习重点 3 | 通过电影内容,了解国际通用的分级制度

学习重点 4 | 列举并用英语介绍经典名片

和朋友聊电影

"Life was like a box of chocolate, you never know what you're gonna get.（人生就像一盒巧克力，你永远不知道下一颗是什么味道？）"这句话不就是在电影《阿甘正传》中大家耳熟能详的那句话吗？

从电影中我们可以学到能在生活中实际利用的英语，也因为电影有声音、角色和情节，我们更容易学习和记住发音、单词、句型！要跟别人用英语来聊电影，我们必须先知道各种类型的电影用英语怎么说。

实用单词　　　MP3 06-01

action [ˈækʃən] n 动作	It is interesting to find heroes in **action films** are getting older. 很有趣的是动作片中的英雄年龄越来越老了。 ※ hero 英雄的复数是"heroes"而不是"heros"。
animation [ˌænəˈmeʃən] n 动画	Computer-animated technology was first used in **animation** movies in 1995. 电脑动画技术在 1995 年首度在动画电影中使用。
comedy [ˈkɑmədɪ] n 喜剧	**Comedy** films bring laughter to the audience. 喜剧片带给观众欢乐。
romantic comedy [rəˈmæntɪk ˈkɑmədɪ] n 浪漫喜剧	Most girls love **romantic comedies** because of happy endings. 因为完美结局，大部分的女孩都喜欢浪漫爱情剧。
drama [ˈdrɑmə] n 剧情	This **drama film** tells the story of a single father. 这部剧情片是讲述有关单亲父亲的故事。
film noir [fɪlm nwar] n 写实片	Smoking is a common scene in **film noir**. 抽烟的场景在写实片中很常见。
horror [ˈhɔrɚ] n 恐怖	**Horror** movies often have some elements that scare us. 恐怖片中通常有一些吓坏我们的要素。
science fiction [ˈsaɪəns ˈfɪkʃən] n 科幻	**Science fiction** films are mostly about time and space travel. 科幻片大都是时间与太空旅行。
suspense [səˈspɛns] n 悬疑	Alfred Hitchcock successfully built tension in his **suspense** movies. 希区柯克成功地在他的悬疑电影中制造出紧张气氛。
western [ˈwɛstɚn] n 西部	Ranches, frontier towns, and saloons are settings for **western** films. 牧场、边境城镇与酒吧是西部片的场景。

Lesson 6

cinema、film、movie 我该使用哪个词？
谈论"电影"的时候，三个都可以指电影，cinema 指电影院。film 跟 movie 通用，film 为英式英语，而 movie 为美式用语。

🎵 MP3 06-02

对话情境

A：What's your favorite type of movies?

B：Of course, romantic comedies.

A：Me too.

B：Like most girls, we both do like romantic comedies.

A：Yes! They are like the escape because we can get away from real life.

B：And happy endings!

A：We can live happily ever after!

B：Exactly!

A：你最喜欢的电影类型是什么？

B：当然是浪漫喜剧片。

A：我也是。

B：跟大部分的女孩一样，我们都喜欢浪漫喜剧片。

A：是的！这类电影像是逃离，因为我们可以逃离现实生活。

B：还有大团圆结局！

A：我们可以从此幸福快乐地生活着！

B：没错！

实用单词

🎵 MP3 06-03

- **favorite type of movies** 喜欢的电影类型 → 形容词 + 名词
- **of course** 当然 → 副词短语
  ▶ 用来修饰整个句子，做加强语气用，替代用词有 absolutely（绝对地），相反词为 of course not。
- **escape** 逃脱、逃离 → 名词
  ▶ 动词 = run away
- **real life** 现实生活 → 形容词 + 名词当复合名词用
- **happy endings** 大团圆结局 → 形容词 + 名词当复合名词用
- **...live happily ever after.**
  ……从此过着幸福快乐的生活。→ 动词 + 副词
  ▶ 是童话故事中常用的结尾句子

语法教室

❶ of course（当然）与 of course not（当然不）的用法

Can you give me a hand? ⟶ **Of course!**
你能帮我吗？　　　　　　　　当然！（我很乐意）

Did you hear what he said? ⟶ **Of course!**
你有听到他说的吗？　　　　　当然有！（怎么可能没听到）

Would you mind passing me the salt? ⟶ **Of course not!**
你不介意递给我盐吧？　　　　当然不介意！

❷ because of 和 because 的用法

之前我们学过的"糨糊"连接词的用法，because 因为语意与语法上都无法单独存在，所以必须附属主要从句。

Because the earthquake occurred last night. (×)
因为昨晚发生地震。（错误句）

句型

- Because of + 名词 , 主语 + 动词
- Because + 主语 + 动词（附属从句）, 主语 + 动词（主要从句）
- 主语 + 动词 because of + 名词
- 主语 + 动词（主要从句）because + 主语 + 动词（附属从句）

例句

Because of the earthquake yesterday, there is a shortage of drinking water.
= Because the earthquake occurred yesterday, there is a shortage of drinking water.
= There is a shortage of drinking water because of the earthquake yesterday.
= There is a shortage of drinking water because the earthquake occurred yesterday.
因为昨天发生地震，所以饮用水不足。

> **注意**
> because 放句中，前面不可有逗号

另外要记得，虽然中文常说"因为……所以……"，但在英语中，because（因为）跟 although（尽管、虽然）不能放在一起使用！

Although I was late, but I was admitted. (×)
虽然我迟到了，我还是可以进入。（错误句）

以"虽然我迟到了，我还是可以进入"举例来说，正确说法为：
Although I was late, I was admitted.
= Although I was late, yet I was admitted.
= I was admitted although I was late.

Unit 2 讨论喜欢的电影

阅读下列说明人们为什么喜欢动作片的相关文章。

Tomorrow, I need to give a talk in front of everyone, and I feel nervous. That is stressful. Some studies told us[1] stress is the main reason for people to enjoy* action movies. We may feel stressed but excited to chase bad guys or to be chased* by bad guys. Furthermore, we know it is not a real situation but controlled one. The good guy will win in the end. They also will end soon, probably* 90 to 120 minutes. After all, we have the chance to identify* ourselves as the heroes in action movies. We can be so confident and courageous. Action movies do help us to better handle the stressful situation in our daily life.

明天，我必须在大家面前说话，我感觉好紧张。那就是压力。一些研究显示，压力是人们喜欢看动作片的主要原因。我们可能必须去追坏人或被坏人追，虽然有压力，但是会感觉很刺激。再者，我们知道这一切不是真的，而且能控制情境。好人最终会赢。电影也很快会播完，可能 90～120 分钟。毕竟我们有机会把自己与动作片中的英雄联系起来。我们可以像他们一样有自信又勇敢。动作片让我们更能释放日常生活中的压力。

实用单词

♪ MP3 06-04

nervous [ˈnɝvəs] a 紧张的
I have butterflies in my stomach; that means I am **nervous**.
我的胃里有蝴蝶，这表示我很紧张。

stress [strɛs] n 压力
In our life, **stress** is normal. 在我们的生活中，压力是正常的。

stressed [strɛst] a 有压力的
When talking with my boss, I feel **stressed**.
跟老板谈话时，我觉得很紧张。

in the end ph 最后
In the end, they overcame tremendous* difficulties.
最后，他们克服了巨大的困难。

identify [aɪˈdɛntəˌfaɪ] v 变成
It is common that[2] we **identify** ourselves with memories.
我们常使用记忆来认同自我。

confident [ˈkɑnfədənt] a 有自信的
courageous [kəˈredʒəs] a 勇敢的
When meeting challenges*, we need to be[3] **confident** and **courageous**.
面对挑战时，我们必须自信且勇敢。

the stressful situation ph 有压力的情况
During **a stressful situation**, we need to give more support to rescue workers.
在充满压力的情况下，我们必须给予救难人员更多的支持。

对话情境 🎵 MP3 06-05

A: Hey, action movies help us to handle stress in daily life!
B: Is it true?
A: Yeah, that article says we feel confident and courageous when watching action films.
B: I feel more❹ confident and courageous when riding on the roller coaster.
A: Correct! That's the common thing that the ride and action films offer us, excitement and relaxation.
B: Why?
A: They are both in the controlled situation and short.
B: You talked me into it.

A：嘿，动作片帮助我们释放日常生活的压力！
B：真的吗？
A：是的，这篇文章说我们在看动作片时都会感觉自信和勇敢。
B：我在坐过山车时感觉更自信更勇敢了。
A：没错！这就是过山车和动作片提供给我们的刺激与放松！
B：为什么？
A：它们都是在控制情境并且时间短。
B：你说服我了。

实用单词 🎵 MP3 06-06

roller coaster ph 过山车	His life has been a **roller coaster**. 他的人生就像是过山车一样。
excitement [ɪkˈsaɪtmənt] n 刺激	Students shared their **excitement** by reading aloud. 学生们大声分享他们的兴奋。
relaxation [ˌrilæksˈeʃən] n 放松	Rita discovered the **relaxation** from a trip to Australia. 澳洲之行让瑞塔很放松。
...talk someone into it ph 说服	It was foolish of him to let her **talked** him **into it**. 他愚蠢地相信了她。

实用句型

❶ **Some studies told us + that 从句**
一些研究显示……

❷ **it is common + that 从句** 通常……

❸ **we need to be** 我们必须……

❹ **I feel more...** 我感觉更……

单词补充 🎵 MP3 06-07

★ **enjoy** [ɪnˈdʒɔɪ] v 欣赏
★ **chase** [tʃes] v 追逐
★ **probably** [ˈprɑbəblɪ] ad 大概
★ **identify** [aɪˈdɛntəˌfaɪ] v 辨别，确认
★ **tremendous** [trɪˈmɛndəs] a 巨大的
★ **challenge** [ˈtʃælɪndʒ] n / v 挑战
★ **aloud** [əˈlaʊd] ad 大声地
★ **discover** [dɪsˈkʌvɚ] v 发现

认识国外的电影分级制度

欧美一些国家,电影分级制度会将电影分为五级:
- 普遍级 / G:一般观众皆可观看。
- 保护级 / PG:部分内容不适合儿童观看,儿童观看需父母陪伴辅导。
- 辅导级 / PG-13:未满 13 岁的儿童不得观看。
- 限制级 / R:未满 17 岁不得观看。
- 禁止级 /NC-17:未满 17 岁禁止观看。

The Motion Picture Association of America(美国电影协会,简称 MPAA)的 film-rating system(电影分级系统):

G — General audiences; all ages admitted
适合一般观众;所有年龄层皆可观赏

PG — Parental guidance suggested; some material may not be suitable for children.
需要父母辅导;有些内容不适合小孩

PG-13 — Parents strongly cautioned; some material may be inappropriate for pre-teenagers.
父母必须注意;有些内容不适合未达青少年年龄的孩子

R — Restricted; under 17 requires accompanying parent or adult guardian.
限制级;17 岁以下必须由父母或成年监护人陪同

NC-17 — No one 17 and under admitted
17 岁以下不得观看

《小黄人》是一部美国出品的电脑动画喜剧片，它让全球各个年龄层的影迷大为疯狂，但是在分级上《小黄人》是辅导级（PG）电影，并不适合六岁以下的儿童观看，下列的文章说明了为什么。

ABC DAILY

Several articles reported Minions hits $1 billion at worldwide* box office. There are fans from different cultures and age groups.

The story is simply about three minions, Kevin, Bob, and Stuart. All minions were born for their evil master, and when they found they have no one to serve in an icy cave, they became depressed. Kevin, Bob, and Stuart were sent to find their master.

Why is this entertaining film not suitable for young children under six? It is because some material* in the film are not suitable for children under six. There are themes of crime, suicide, natural disasters, drug and alcohol abuse, death, serious illness, family breakdown*, and animal cruelty. These may adversely affect young children or even adults*.

In addition, violence is also an important issue in the film. Normally, violence such as punches and shooting in movies make children feel less sensitive to the use of violence in real life. Thus, it has been suggested that this movie is most suitable for children aged over six.

许多文章都报道《小黄人》在全世界票房缔造了 10 亿美元的纪录。《小黄人》有来自不同文化与年龄层的粉丝。

故事很简单，是关于三个小黄人凯文、鲍勃和斯图尔特的故事。所有的小黄人都是为了服侍邪恶的主人而生，在他们发现自己没有主人可以服侍时，小黄人觉得很沮丧。凯文、鲍勃和斯图尔特就被派去寻找主人。

为什么这部具娱乐性的电影不适合六岁以下的儿童观看？因为影片中有些内容不适合六岁以下的儿童观看。有犯罪、自杀、天灾、药物与酗酒、死亡、严重疾病、家庭破碎与虐待动物等场景。这些可能会对年纪小的小孩甚至成年人有负面影响。

除此之外，暴力也是影片中的一个重要议题。通常，影片中的暴力，像痛殴与射杀会让小孩对现实生活中的暴力的使用无感。因此这部影片据此建议比较适合六岁以上的儿童。

语法教室

动词过去式、现在式与现在完成式的使用

过去式 发生在过去时间与状态的动词
主语加过去式动词
She **did** her homework **a few minutes ago.** 她几分钟前在做功课。
She **ran** into an old friend **yesterday.** 她昨天遇到一位老友。

现在式 主语 + 动词原形，陈述事实与现在的状态。
主语 + 动词原形（主语为第三人称单数时，动词加 **s** 或 **es**）
She **does** her homework. 她做功课。
She **runs** into an old friend. 她遇到一位老友。

现在完成式 发生在过去时间与状态持续到现在的动词
主语 + has / have + 过去分词
She **has done** her homework. 她已经完成功课。
She **has contacted** her friend in Sydney. 她已经联络她在悉尼的朋友。

注意 在讲述故事与描述影片场景时，除了描述事实场景，使用现在式外，其他许多场景因为都是已经发生的动作或状态，常使用过去式与现在完成式动词。

实用单词

 MP3 06-08

worldwide box office ph 全世界票房	These are top 100 movies at the **worldwide box office**. 这些是全球票房前 100 名的大电影。
age group ph 年龄层	This product targets* consumer at the **age group** under 20. 此产品锁定年龄层在 20 岁以下的消费者。
an icy cave ph 冰洞	Snow covered* the **icy cave**. 雪覆盖在冰洞上。
suitable [ˈsutəbl] a 合适的	Fruit and vegetables are **suitable** foods for rabbits. 蔬果是适合兔子的食物。
crime [kraɪm] n 犯罪	The community watch plan helps to reduce* and deter **crime**. 邻里守望相助计划有助减少与遏阻犯罪。
suicide [ˈsuəˌsaɪd] n 自杀	**Suicide** is considered as a waste of life. 自杀被视为浪费生命。
drug and alcohol abuse ph 药物与酒精滥用 **family breakdown** ph 家庭破碎	**Drug and alcohol abuse** commonly leads to **family breakdown**. 药物与酒精滥用常常导致家庭破碎。
animal cruelty ph 虐待动物	**Animal cruelty** includes the failure to take care of an animal. 虐待动物包括未好好照顾动物。
violence [ˈvaɪələns] n 暴力	This campaign* aims to prevent* **violence**. 这个活动的目标是预防暴力。
punch [pʌntʃ] n / v 痛殴	Because of his betrayal*, I would like to give him a **punch**. 因为他的背叛，我想揍他一拳。
shooting [ˈʃutɪŋ] n 射杀	In the **shooting**, two men died. 在枪击中，有两个人死亡。

单词补充
MP3 06-09

* **worldwide** [ˈwɝldwaɪd] a 遍及全球的
* **material** [məˈtɪrɪəl] n 素材
* **breakdown** [ˈbrekˌdaʊn] n 崩坏
* **adult** [ˈədʌlt] a 成年人
* **target** [ˈtɑrgɪt] n 目标
* **cover** [ˈkʌvɚ] v 覆盖
* **reduce** [rɪˈdjus] v 减少
* **campaign** [kæmˈpen] n 活动, 运动
* **prevent** [prɪˈvɛnt] v 预防, 防止
* **betray** [bɪˈtre] v 背叛

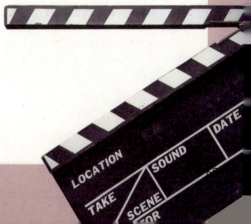

值得一看再看的经典名片

Best movies of all time（经典名片）值得一看再看，在此我们列出 8 部各类电影的经典名片，并且提供剧情摘要，让您可以与人畅所欲言地谈电影。

007, James Bond Films
"007"系列电影
The films portrait stories of a British secret agent working for MI6 with the codename, 007.
电影描述为 MI6 工作的英国情报员 007 的故事。

Star Wars《星球大战》系列电影
The series films portrait the starship missions in space journey.
此系列电影描述在星际旅程中的太空船任务。

Transformer《变形金刚》系列电影
The film tells about the battles between the noble Autobots and the devious Decepticons.
电影讲述正义的汽车人与邪恶派之间的战役。

Psycho《惊魂记》
The film tells about the killing of Marion Crane, a real estate secretary, by the mentally ill woman, Norma.
电影讲述房地产秘书 Marion Crane 被患有精神病 Norma 所杀害的故事。

Schindler's List《辛德勒的名单》
A German businessman Schindler, also a Nazi Party member, plans to hire over a thousand Jewish workers for his factory in order to protect them.
一位德国的生意人，也是纳粹党员辛德勒，计划雇用 1000 名犹太工人在他的工厂工作，以保护他们。

The Devil Wears Prada
《穿着普拉达的女王》
It is about the job of an aspiring journalist fresh out of Northwestern University at a fashion magazine.
这是有关一位刚从西北大学新闻系毕业的学生在一家流行杂志的工作经历。

Inside Out《头脑特攻队》
The film tells about a young girl, Riley, and her inner emotions—Joy, Sadness, Fear, Anger, and Disgust.
电影讲述莱莉与其内在情绪：乐乐、忧忧、惊惊、怒怒与厌厌的故事。

Lesson 7
那些电影教我的英语！

学习重点 1	用英语邀请别人看电影
学习重点 2	买票、买爆米花、看电影
学习重点 3	观看国外的电影颁奖典礼实况转播
学习重点 4	熟悉并引用经典电影台词

Unit 1 邀约看电影

在 Lesson 6 中,我们学习了电影的类型、分级与经典名片,知道如何与别人用英语聊自己喜欢的电影,接下来,我们来看看电影教会我们的英语还有哪些。首先,看电影一定要有伴,我们可以利用以下两则对话中的范例来邀请别人看电影。

对话情境

♪ MP3 07-01

A: Hey, Tim, Tammy and I are going to take kids to see *The Good Dinosaur tonight*. <u>Would you like to</u> come?❶

B: When?

A: We're <u>going to</u>❷ see the 20:35 show.

B: <u>That sounds good to me</u>.❸ Should I meet you all at the theater?

A: Terrific! We'll meet you there.

A:嗨,蒂姆,泰咪和我今晚要带孩子去看《恐龙当家》。你要去吗?

B:什么时候?

A:我们要看 20:35 分的电影。

B:可以。我是否跟你们在戏院碰面?

A:太好了!我们那里见。

实用句型

❶ **Would you like to + 动词?/ Would you like + 名词?**
你想要 _____?

Would you like to <u>go biking</u>? 你要去骑自行车吗?
Would you like <u>some tea</u>? 要喝点茶吗?

❷ **be going to _____ 打算去 _____**
We are going to <u>San Francisco</u> this summer. 今年夏天我们打算去旧金山。

❸ **That sounds good / great to me.**
太棒了。/ 太好了。(在同意对话者提议、计划时使用)

例如:如果你的朋友提议:Do you want to go for a ride with me? 你要跟我一起去兜风吗?
你就可以欣然同意地说:That sounds great to me. 或 That sounds good to me.

Lesson 7

对话情境 🎵 MP3 07-02

A: Hi, Tim.
B: What's up, Sally?
A: I was wondering if① you have any plans for this weekend. Do you want to see *13 Hours: The Secret Soldiers of Benghazi* with me?
B: I'd love to.
A: What time would be good for you?②
B: I will be available after 7:00 pm.
A: OK.

A：嗨，蒂姆。
B：莎莉，你好吗？
A：我在想你周末有没有什么计划。你要不要跟我去看《危机13小时》？
B：我愿意。
A：你什么时间有空？
B：我晚上七点之后有空。
A：好的。

如果受邀去看电影，却去不了，要如何有礼貌地拒绝呢？接下来看下一个对话情境。

对话情境 🎵 MP3 07-03

A: Hi, Tim. Do you want to see *13 Hours: The Secret Soldiers of Benghazi* with me?
B: Thank you, Sally, but I am sorry. I won't be able to make it.
A: Okay, no problem. We'll do it another time.③

A：嗨，蒂姆。你要不要跟我去看《危机13小时》？
B：谢谢你，莎莉，但是很抱歉，我没办法去。
A：没关系。我们下次去。

❶ I was wondering if _____ . 我在想你是否 _____ 。
与 **Could you / Would you** 的意思差不多，但较为委婉。

❷ What time would be good for you to _____ ?
你什么时候有空 _____ ?（询问对方时间的礼貌用法）

❸ Okay, no problem. We'll do it another time. 没关系。我们下次去。
也可以说：**Let's take a rain check.** 下次再约。（有此约定但没有确切时间）

注意

- What's up?
  朋友之间的打招呼、问候，等于 What's new? 及 Hi。

- Thank you for the invitation, but I am sorry. I'll not be able to make it.
  谢谢你的邀请，但是抱歉，我去不了。（拒绝邀约时使用，记得要感谢邀请）

Unit 2 看电影时，一定要做的事

看电影时的第一件事，就是要买票，怎么用英语来买票呢？

对话情境

♪ MP3 07-04

A: Hi, <u>may I help you?</u>❶

B: Yes, two adult and two child tickets for the 20:35 show of *The Good Dinosaur*.

A: <u>Where would you like to sit?</u>❷

B: We would like to sit in row D, seats 1-4. <u>How much would that be?</u>❸

A: That would be $40 dollars.

A：嗨，需要我为您服务吗？

B：是的，两张大人和两张小孩 20:35 分的《恐龙当家》电影票。

A：您想坐哪里？

B：我们想坐 D 排 1~4 号。多少钱？

A：总共 40 元钱。

实用句型

❶ **May I help you?**
需要我为您服务吗？

或可以说 How can I help you? 我要如何协助您？
都是店员招呼顾客时常用的话。

❷ **Where would you like to sit?**
您想坐哪？（询问选择座位时用）

We only have last few seats available. Where would you like to seat?
我们只剩几个座位。您想坐哪？

❸ **How much would that be?**
多少钱？

也可以问：How much?
或 How much is it?

- couple ['kʌpl] n 情侣
- moviegoer ['muvɪgoɚ] n 常看电影的人
- counter ['kaʊntɚ] n 柜台
- microphone ['maɪkrəˌfon] n 扩音器
- full fare ticket ph 全票

看电影一定要来一桶爆米花（**popcorn**）加点 **butter**（奶油）或 **caramel**（焦糖），所以看电影也称为 **popcorn time**（爆米花时间），爆米花是如何与电影产生关系的呢？先阅读下面一篇文章。

Popcorn became the main snack* in the beginning of 20 century. But popcorn was once banned* in theaters because it made a mess* and was thought to distract* moviegoers*. Popcorn during that time was sold mainly by street vendors*. People needed to go outside theaters to buy popcorn.

Owners* of theaters later understood that they could make the profit by selling popcorn inside the theaters. After the first electric popcorn machine* was introduced in 1925, machines were moved into the lobby* of theaters.

Even during the Great Depression, people could still enjoy a movie and popcorn with a nickel. Filling*, cheap, and tasty popcorn increased not only in sales but also in popularity* at theaters since then. Now popcorn and movie experience are integrated*.

　　爆米花在 20 世纪初成为风行的零食。但是电影院曾经一度禁止食用爆米花，因为容易造成脏乱，并且被认为会让看电影的人不专心。那时候，爆米花主要是由街上的摊贩来贩售的。人们必须到戏院外才能买到爆米花。

　　后来，电影院老板也在电影院内卖爆米花来牟利。在 1925 年第一台电子爆米花机问世后，机器就可以移动到电影院大厅。

　　甚至在大萧条时，人们还是可以以 5 美分的价格享受一部电影和爆米花。有饱足感、便宜与美味的爆米花不仅在电影院内增加销量，受欢迎度也水涨船高。现在爆米花和看电影已经密不可分了。

★ 提供几个文中要注意的地方：❶ The Great Depression 指 "1929—1933 年的全球经济大衰退"。❷ 比起 delicious，英语母语人士较常使用 tasty 来形容食物的美味。

单词补充　　♪ MP3 07-05

* ★ snack [snæk] n 零食
* ★ ban [bæn] v 禁止
* make a mess ph 弄脏
* ★ distract [dɪˈstrækt] v 分散、转移
* moviegoer ph 看电影的人
* street vendors ph 街上摊贩
* ★ owner [ˈonɚ] n 所有人
* electric popcorn machine ph 电子爆米花机
* lobby [ˈlɑbɪ] n 大厅
* filling [ˈfɪlɪŋ] a 有饱足感的
* popularity [ˌpɑpjəˈlærətɪ] n 受欢迎程度
* integrate [ˈɪntəˌgret] v 整合

接下来，我们要使用上页表格中的单词与短语练习再写一篇以电影与爆米花为主题的文章。

Can you imagine watching a movie without popcorn? No way! After all, watching a movie is popcorn time.

In fact, once in a while, popcorn was banned at theaters. Why? It was because eating popcorn can easily make a mess and distract other moviegoers.

In addition, moviegoers needed to go outside theaters to buy popcorn since popcorn in the beginning was sold by street vendors. It was not until theater owners understood they can also make a profit by selling popcorn that popcorn was sold at theaters.

Popcorn became the main snack food in the early 20th Century after the first electric popcorn machine was invented. Popcorn machines then were able to be pushed into the lobby of theaters. Popcorn has been affordable. Even during the Great Depression, people could use a nickel to buy a movie ticket and a pack of popcorn.

We refer movie watching as popcorn time now, and that proves popcorn has been a part of movie watching experience.

你可以想象看电影没有爆米花吗？绝不！毕竟，看电影就是爆米花时间。

事实上，一度，在电影院里不能吃爆米花。为什么？因为吃爆米花容易制造脏乱并且分散看电影人的注意力。

此外，看电影的人必须到电影院外才能买到爆米花，因为一开始时，只有街上小贩在卖爆米花。一直到戏院老板了解到他们也可以卖爆米花来牟利，戏院才卖起爆米花。

爆米花在第一台电子爆米花机器发明后，在20世纪初成为主要的零食。爆米花机被推入到了戏院大厅。爆米花一直是人们买得起的零食。甚至在大萧条时，人们也可以用五分钱买到一张电影票与一包爆米花。我们现在把看电影称为爆米花时间，这显示爆米花与看电影已经是一体的。

写作小教室

在第二篇文章中，除了将第一篇文章的用词以其他可以取代的词性、形式、结构等做出区别外，最大的不同点在于问题的使用，像一开头的 **Can you imagine...** 及 **Why?** 等问句。

使用问句是吸引读者的技巧，但是给了问题后一定要给答案，否则读的人会觉得易混淆。文章中的 **No way!**（绝不）及 **It was because...**（是因为……）等句子就是答案句。

注意

关于"买爆米花"时会用到的句子

- 找寻卖爆米花的地点
  Where can I buy popcorn?
  哪里有卖爆米花的？

- 买的时候的口味选择
  Salt and butter, sugar and butter, or caramel?
  盐和奶油、糖和奶油还是焦糖？

- **size of popcorn** 爆米花大小
  small, medium, large, extra large
  小、中、大、加大

Unit 3 电影首映及相关奖项

我们也要来看看电影首映及相关奖项的词汇与用法。
- premiere（首映式），即 the first public performance（首次公开演出）
- a heavy promotional schedule（紧锣密鼓的宣传行程）
- red carpet（红地毯）
- blockbuster（卖座巨片）

熟悉相关单词与短语后，我们来阅读下列两篇短文：

Tom Cruise appeared at the New York City premiere of his next summer blockbuster, *Mission: Impossible - Rogue Nation*. He wore a dark blue suit with a tie and joined on the red carpet by co-stars* and celebrity* fans. The superstar will soon begin a heavy promotional schedule for the movie.

汤姆·克鲁斯出现在他下一部夏天卖座巨片《碟中谍：法外国度》于纽约的首映式。他穿着深蓝色西装，打着领带，与共同演出的巨星与名人粉丝一起走上红地毯。巨星将很快地开始该影片紧锣密鼓的宣传行程。

The well-known Japanese master and Director, Hayao Miyazaki, received the Academy Honorary Award for his contributions in the past years to the motion picture industry.
This was the second Oscar statuette* given to Miyazaki besides his first one in 2013 for the best feature animated film, "Spirited Away."
"Hayao Miyazaki has deeply influenced animation* forever, inspiring generations* of artists..." commented by John Lasseter, Chief Creative Officer at Walt Disney* and Pixar Animation Studios* who presented the award to Miyazaki in person*.

知名的大师、导演宫崎骏因为过去多年来对电影产业的贡献，获得了奥斯卡终身成就奖。
这是宫崎骏所获得的第二个奥斯卡小金人；在 2013 年，他因为《千与千寻》而赢得他的第一个奥斯卡金像奖最佳影片奖项。
亲自颁发奖项给宫崎骏的迪士尼与皮克斯动画工作室总监约翰莱斯特说："宫崎骏对动画有深远的影响，他激励了数个世代的艺术家……"

单词补充　♪ MP3 07-06

- ★ co-star [ˈko͵stɑr] n./v. 联合主演
- ★ celebrity [sɪˈlɛbrətɪ] n. 名人
- ★ statuette [͵stætʃuˈɛt] n. 小雕像
- ★ animation [͵ænəˈmeʃən] n. 动画片
- ★ generation [͵dʒɛnəˈreʃən] n. 世代
- Walt Disney ph. 华特迪士尼
- Pixar Animation Studios ph. 皮克斯动画工作室
- in person ph. 亲自

77

每一年电影界的年度盛事为：奥斯卡金像奖颁奖典礼。英语为 **The Oscars**，也称为 **Academy Award**（学院奖）、**Academy Award of Merit**（学院功绩奖），在这场年度盛会上，能够入围奖项对于电影工作者来说就是一种肯定。

颁奖典礼开始前，会有红地毯的走秀，全世界都在期待看到明星们在红毯上的穿着与打扮，也有不少时尚博主或评论者，在看完之后，他们会发表个人对于明星穿着的意见。而在颁奖的时候，会有颁奖者先宣布入围者（**nominees**），再公布得奖者（**winner**），之后得奖者会上台致辞表示感谢。

Best Motion Picture of the Year	年度最佳影片奖
Best Performance by an Actor* in a Leading Role*	最佳男主角奖
Best Performance by an Actress* in a Leading Role	最佳女主角奖
Best Performance by an Actor in a Supporting Role*	最佳男配角奖
Best Performance by an Actress in a Supporting Role	最佳女配角奖
Best Achievement in Directing	最佳导演奖
Best Writing, Original Screenplay	最佳原创剧本奖
Best Writing, Adapted Screenplay	最佳改编剧本奖
Best Achievement in Cinematography*	最佳摄影奖
Best Achievement in Costume Design	最佳服装设计奖
Best Achievement in Sound Mixing	最佳混音奖
Best Achievement in Film Editing	最佳剪辑奖
Best Achievement in Sound Editing	最佳音效剪辑奖
Best Achievement in Visual* Effects	最佳视觉效果奖
Best Achievement in Makeup and Hairstyling	最佳化妆与发型设计奖

单词补充 ♪ MP3 07-07

- ★ **actor** ['æktɚ] n 男演员
- ★ **leading role** pn 主角
- ★ **actress** ['æktrɪs] n 女演员
- ★ **supporting role** pn 配角
- ★ **cinematography** [ˌsɪnəmə'tɑgrəfɪ] n 电影艺术
- ★ **visual** ['vɪʒuəl] a 视觉的
- ★ **documentary** [ˌdɑkjə'mɛntərɪ] n 纪录片
- ★ **honorary** ['ɑnərɛrɪ] a 名誉上的
- ★ **commendation** [ˌkɑmən'deʃən] n 表扬
- ★ **humanitarian** [hjuˌmænə'tɛrɪən] a 人道主义的

Best Achievement in Music Written for Motion Pictures, Original Song	最佳原创歌曲奖
Best Achievement in Music Written for Motion Pictures, Original Score	最佳原创音乐奖
Best Short Film, Animated	最佳动画短片奖
Best Short Film, Live Action	最佳纪实短片奖
Best Documentary★, Short Subject	最佳纪录短片奖
Best Documentary, Feature	最佳纪录长片奖
Best Foreign Language Film of the Year	年度最佳外语片奖
Best Animated Feature Film of the Year	年度最佳动画长片奖
Best Achievement in Production Design	最佳艺术设计奖
Honorary★ Award	奥斯卡终身成就奖
Award of Commendation★	成就表扬奖
Jean Hersholt Humanitarian★ Award	琼·赫肖尔特人道主义奖
Scientific and Engineering Award	科学与工程奖
Technical Achievement Award	科技成果奖
Gordon E. Sawyer Award	戈登·E·索耶奖

Unit 4 电影中的佳句

电影中总有一些佳句让我们一再重诉、回味，有哪些范例呢？ 🎵 MP3 07-08

A boy's best friend is his mother.
男孩的挚友是他的母亲。
Psycho《惊魂记》（1960）

Carpe diem. Seize the day, boys. Make your lives extraordinary.
及时行乐。过好每一天，同学们。让你的生活变得非凡。
Dead Poets Society《死亡诗社》（1989）

Whoever saves one life, saves the world entire.
拯救一条生命的人，就拯救了全世界。
Schindler's List《辛德勒的名单》（1993）

If I'm too good for him, then how come I'm not with him?
如果他配不上我，那为什么我们没在一起？
Clueless《独领风骚》（1995）

I've got a very bad feeling about this.
我有一个极度不好的预感。
Star Wars《星球大战》

You have to accept that there are certain things you won't understand right away.
你必须接受有些特定的事物是你无法马上理解的。
Transformer《变形金刚》（2007）

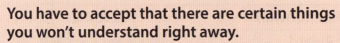

Be serious. You are not trying. You are whining.
严肃些。你试都没试，只是在抱怨。
The Devil Wears Prada《穿着普拉达的女王》（2006）

Be nice to people because the world can be a very difficult place and we all need a little help sometimes.
善待人们，这世界谁不会遇到困难，我们也会有需要帮助的时候。
Minion《小黄人》（2015）

点餐三部曲

It's time to eat! 大快朵颐的时间到了。我们要来学习与食物有关的英语，先来看一下菜单。以下列举一般餐厅 **menu** 中常见的词汇：

starters（开胃菜、前菜）、**soup**（汤品）、**salads**（沙拉）、**entrees**（主菜）、**smokehouse foods**（烧烤类）、**sandwiches**（三明治）、**burgers**（汉堡）、**desserts**（甜点）、**Kids Meals**［儿童餐会标示 "**for kids under 12**（限 12 岁以下）"］、**beverage**（饮料）

点餐可以分成三部曲：先点饮料，再点餐点，接着要账单，我们来看看这三部曲如何进行。

点餐首部曲

♪ MP3 08-01

A：Hi! How many of you?
B：Table for three.
A：This way, please. My name is Veronica, and I am your waitress today. What would you like to drink first?
B：I would like to have a glass of Long Island Iced Tea, coke and apple juice for the lady and the kid.
A：Do you need Kids Menu?
B：Yes, please.
A：I will be right back with a Kids Menu and your drinks.

A：嗨！有几位？
B：三位。
A：这边请。我是维罗妮卡，您今天的服务生。您要先来点饮料吗？
B：我要杯长岛冰茶，女士要可乐，小孩要苹果汁。
A：您需要儿童菜单吗？
B：是的，请。
A：我马上拿儿童菜单和饮料给您。

▶ 从对话中，我们可以学到：

❶ How many of you?
   = How many of you will be? = How many people are in your party?
   = 有几位？
❷ 回复人数的时候可以说：**Table for three**（三个人），或直接给个数字：**Three**（三人）。
❸ **Yes, please.**（是的，请。）也可以说：**Yeah** 或 **Sure**。不需要的话，就说：**No, thank you.**（不，谢谢您。）

Lesson 8

语法教室

❶ How many 与 How much 的用法

How many + 可数名词?
复数名词 + are there?
How many + 复数名词 + 助动词 + 主语 + 动词?

How much + 不可数名词 + is there?
How many + 复数名词 + 助动词 + 主语 + 动词?

Long Island Iced Tea
长岛冰茶
长岛冰茶源自纽约长岛，是非常受欢迎的调味酒，之所以称为茶，是因为没有使用茶却能调出茶的颜色。

❷ 如何数物质名词?

数物质名词时，要加上量词：

<u>a glass of</u> milk 一杯牛奶 / <u>a bottle of</u> water 一瓶水 / <u>a cup of</u> tea 一杯茶 /
<u>a piece of</u> toast 一片吐司 / <u>a pound of</u> sugar 一磅糖

点餐二部曲

♪ MP3 08-02

A: Are you ready to order or do you need a few more minutes?

B: We are ready to order. We'll start with a salad and soup.

A: What kind of dressing would you like?

B: What do you have?

A: We have Blue Cheese, Caesar, French, Honey Dijon, Italian or Thousand Island dressing.

B: Blue Cheese, please.

A: How about your soup? Clam chowder or vegetable soup?

B: We would like to have vegetable soup.

A: What would you like to have for the main course?

B: A cheese and ham sandwich and steak. Macaroni cheese for the kid.

A: How would you like your steak done?

B: Medium.

A: Would you like to have some dessert?

B: Ice cream and carrot cake.

A: 您已经准备好要点餐，还是需要再等几分钟？
B: 我们已经准备好要点餐。先来沙拉和汤。
A: 您要什么沙拉酱？
B: 有什么选择？
A: 我们有蓝起司、恺撒、法式、蜂蜜芥末、意式或千岛沙拉酱。
B: 请给我蓝起司。
A: 您的汤呢？蛤蜊巧达浓汤还是蔬菜汤？
B: 我们要蔬菜汤。
A: 主餐要点什么？
B: 一个火腿起司三明治和牛排。小孩要乳酪通心粉。
A: 您的牛排要几分熟？
B: 五分熟。
A: 要来点甜点吗？
B: 冰淇淋与红萝卜蛋糕。

从点餐三部曲的对话中可以学到几句最常用的会话句：
- **Are you ready to order?** 您已经准备好要点餐了吗？
- **Do you have any question about the menu?** 您对于菜单有任何问题吗？
- **Do you need some more minutes?** 您还需要一点时间吗？
- **What do you have?** 有哪些选择？

What kind of dressing would you like?
您要什么沙拉酱？
dressing 沙拉酱（名词），常见的有：**Blue Cheese**（蓝起司）、**Caesar**（恺撒）、**French**（法式）、**Honey Dijon (mustard)**（蜂蜜芥末）、**Italian**（意式）、**Ranch**（田园）、**Thousand Island**（千岛）

How would you like your steak done?
您的牛排要几分熟？
rare（一分熟）、**medium rare**（三分熟）、**medium**（五分熟）、**medium well**（七分熟）、**well done**（全熟）
在西餐厅，牛排的熟度只有以上选项，为了卫生安全考量，除非特定菜色，餐厅提供的熟度至少为三分，有些餐厅如未指定，也会将牛排熟度烹至三分。

接下来，开始练习实际点餐的对话，请依据您想吃的餐点，填写空格：

A: Are you ready to order or do you need some more minutes?

B: _____. I'll start with salad and soup.

A: What kind of dressing would you like? We have Blue Cheese, Caesar or Thousand Island dressing.

B: _____, please.

A: How about your soup? Clam chowder or vegetable soup?

B: We would like to have _____.

A: What would you like to have for the main course?

B: Steak, _____.

A: Would you like to have some dessert?

B: _____.

A: 您已经准备好要点餐还是需要再等几分钟？

B: 先来沙拉和汤。

A: 您要什么沙拉酱？我们有蓝起司、恺撒或千岛沙拉酱。

B: 请给我_____。

A: 您的汤呢？蛤蜊巧达浓汤还是蔬菜汤？

B: 我们要_____。

A: 主餐要点什么？

B: 牛排，____分熟。

A: 要来点甜点吗？

B:

点餐三部曲

♪ MP3 08-03

A: Can I bring you anything else?
B: No, thank you. Just the bill*, please.
A: Certainly*.
B: How much is the lunch?
A: That's $50.88.
B: Here you are. Thank you very much.
A: You're welcome. Have a nice* day.
B: Thank you, and you have a nice day, too*.

A：您还需要点别的吗？
B：不用，谢谢。只需要给我账单。
A：没问题。
B：午餐多少钱？
A：50.88 美金。
B：给您。非常感谢。
A：不客气。祝您有美好的一天。
B：谢谢，也祝您有美好的一天。

不可不知道的句子有：
- Can I bring you anything else?
  您还需要点别的吗？
- Have a nice day! 祝您有美好的一天。
  可以回应：You have a nice day, too.
  或 Same to you.

单词补充 ♪ MP3 08-04
★ bill [bɪl] n 账单（也称为 check）
★ certainly ['sɝtnlɪ] ad 好的、无疑的
★ nice [naɪs] a 美好的
★ too [tu] ad 也

开胃菜　牛肉　特色料理、本店招牌

沙拉　鸡肉　甜点　饮料

认识食物金字塔

认识食物（getting to know your food）就从认识食物金字塔（food pyramid）开始。

一直到最近，学界根据研究而修正了食物金字塔。想要有健康的身体，在饮食方式上，现在更强调要减少进食红肉、精致的谷类食物，并要减少进食饱和脂肪，多食不饱和脂肪（如植物油），当然最重要的还有每日做适量运动。

单词补充　♪ MP3 08-05

- ★ calorie [ˈkælərɪ] n 卡路里
- ★ diabetes [ˌdaɪəˈbitiz] n 糖尿病
- ★ hypertension [ˌhaɪpɚˈtɛnʃən] n 高血压
- ★ hypotension [ˌhaɪpəˈtɛnʃən] n 低血压
- ★ blood sugar n 血糖
- ★ obesity [oˈbisətɪ] n 肥胖
- ★ overweight [ˌovɚˈwet] a 过重的 n 超重
- ★ Bulimia nervosa n 暴食症
- ★ anorexia [ˌænəˈrɛksɪə] n 厌食症
- ★ constipation [ˌkɑnsəˈpeʃən] n 便秘

学习短文

♪ MP3 08-06

The food pyramid is a concept showing us how to eat healthily every day. The food pyramid consists of* three layers. At the bottom layers of the food pyramid, there are mainly plant foods* such as❶ vegetables, fruit, and grains. These account for* 70% of what we consume, the biggest portion* of our diet*. The plant foods provide us with most our carbohydrates* and fibers*. At least, two servings* of fruit and five servings of vegetables should be consumed* by an adult every day.

The middle layer contains nuts, dairy products, eggs, fish, and meats and provides us protein* and healthy fat*.

The top layer is oils with healthy fat. Small and proper amount of good oils support our heart and brain functions. Do avoid❷* saturated* and trans* fats.

食物金字塔告诉我们如何健康饮食的概念。食物金字塔总共有三层。底层为主要的植物性食物，像蔬菜、水果和谷物。这些占我们日常饮食的最大部分，约为我们所摄取食物的70%。植物性食物提供给我们碳水化合物和纤维。一位成年人每日至少应该摄取两份水果与四份蔬菜。

中间为坚果、乳制品、蛋、鱼和肉，这些提供给我们蛋白质和健康脂肪。

最上层为含健康脂肪的油脂。少量与恰当的良好油脂支持我们心脏与脑部的功能。不过，要避免食用饱和与反式脂肪。

语法教室

consist of 跟 compose of 要如何使用？

consist of（主动）
The Committee <u>consists of</u> five members.
委员会成员有五位。

compose of（被动）
The Committee is <u>composed of</u> five members.
委员会成员有五位。

实用句型

❶ There are mainly ＿＿＿＿ such as ＿＿＿＿
主要有 ＿＿＿＿ 像是 ＿＿＿＿

❷ Do avoid ＿＿＿＿
避免 ＿＿＿＿

单词补充　♪ MP3 08-07

* **consist of** ph. 包含
* **plant foods** ph. 植物性食物
* **account for** ph. 占……
* **portion** ['porʃən] n. 比例
* **diet** ['daɪət] n. 饮食
* **carbohydrate** ph. 碳水化合物
* **fiber** ['faɪbə] n. 纤维
* **serve** [sɜv] n. 份（以蔬菜而言，一份约是一颗棒球的大小）
* **consume** [kən'sjum] v. 摄取
* **protein** ['protin] n. 蛋白质
* **fat** [fæt] n. 脂肪
* **avoid** [ə'vɔɪd] v. 避免
* **saturated** ['sætʃə,retɪd] a. 饱和的
* **trans** [træns] a. （字首）反式的

Unit 3 可持续食物生产与消费

除了知道可持续（sustainability）这个词之外，我们也必须了解不可持续食物的生产与消费会带给地球更多的破坏，下一篇文章就告诉我们为什么要追求可持续食物的生产与消费。

We eat to live, and food is important to us. Food is also an important part of our cultural and economic life. We all know what we eat affects* our health, but we are not well aware of the impact of❶ food we produce and consume on the environment*, such as, the land and water resources* we use generate* pollution*.

In addition, current trend* of food production* and consumption is not sustainable. Today, food production systems often compromise* the capacity* of Earth to produce food in the future. In the future,❷ climate change and the loss of biodiversity* will make food more inaccessible for the poor.

We have seen many different views on sustainability*. Sustainability, strictly speaking, should refer to the rate for us to consume resources that should not exceed* the capacity for Earth to restore them. Only when foods are sustainably produced and consumed are we able to meet challenges* of critical issues* such as food health and security, climate change, and biodiversity.

How can we achieve the goal of❸ sustainable food production and consumption to lower the environmental impact? We need to reduce input, minimize* waste, improve resource management, change consumption pattern, optimize* production output, and facilitate* logistics.

　　我们必须吃东西才能存活，而食物对我们而言，非常重要。食物也是我们文化与经济生活中的重要部分。我们都知道我们吃的东西会影响我们的健康，但是我们并不清楚我们所生产与消费的食物对环境的影响。例如，我们使用的土地与水资源会产生污染。
　　除此之外，目前的食物生产与消费趋势并不可持续。今日，食物生产系统通常都破坏了地球未来生产食物的能力。在未来，气候变迁与丧失生物多样性会让穷人更买不起食物。
　　我们见到许多对于可持续性的不同看法。可持续性，严格地说，指我们所使用资源的速度不能超过地球替换的能力。只有我们在可持续地生产与消费食物时，才能克服关键议题，像是食物卫生与安全、气候变迁与生物多样性等带来的挑战。
　　我们要如何达成可持续食物生产与消费的目标，以减少对环境的影响？我们必须减少投入、降低浪费、改善资源管理、改变消费模式、优化生产产出与促进物流。

实用句型

❶ We are not well aware of the impact of _____ .
我们并不大清楚 _____ 的影响。

❷ In the future, _____ .
在未来 _____ 。

❸ How can we achieve the goal of _____ ?
我们要如何达到 _____ 的目标？

实用单词

♪ MP3 08-08

consume [kənˈsjum] v 消费
→名词为 consumption [kənˈsʌmpʃən]
n 消耗（量）
for example ph 例如（= for instance）
sustainable [səˈstenəbl] a 可持续的
→名词为 sustainability [sə،stenəˈbɪlɪtɪ] 可持续性
strictly speaking ph 严格地说
generally speaking ph 一般而言

- We eat to live. 我们为了生存而吃。
- We live to eat. 我们为了吃而生存。
（美食爱好者会说的话）

在这个主题下，将我们会用到的单词做名词和动词的分类，以便学习。

名词	动词
environment [ɪnˈvaɪrənmənt] 环境	affect [əˈfɛkt] 影响
resource [rɪˈsors] 资源	generate [ˈdʒɛnəˌret] 产生
pollution [pəˈluʃən] 污染	compromise [ˈkɑmprəˌmaɪz] 牺牲、让步
trend [trɛnd] 趋势	exceed [ɪkˈsid] 超过
production [prəˈdʌkʃən] 生产	minimize [ˈmɪnəˌmaɪz] 最少化
capacity [kəˈpæsətɪ] 能力	optimize [ˈɑpəˌmaɪz] 优化
sustainability [sə،stenəˈbɪlɪtɪ] 可持续性	facilitate [fəˈsɪləˌtet] 促进
biodiversity [baɪoˌdaɪˈvɜsətɪ] 生物多样性	
challenge [ˈtʃælɪndʒ] 挑战	
issue [ˈɪʃju] 议题	

Unit 4 当地生产与当地消费

什么是当地生产与当地消费的概念？下一篇短文中有答案。

The Local Food Production Local Consumption Model *　is simple: local people sell foods they produce, both fresh *　and processed, at local markets *.

What are the benefits of this model? Because producers can sell their products directly *　to the consumers in local community, they can reduce the cost of transportation *　as well as the losses of products. Consumers can also pay lower prices.

Moreover, local consumers will not demand *　too much for the look of local produce *. Producers also can contact and communicate with local *　consumers directly. Thus, producers are able to receive *　feedbacks from consumers and then produce foods that local consumers like.

食物在当地生产当地消费的模式很简单：当地人在当地市场销售他们所生产的东西，包括新鲜的与加工的食品。

这种模式有什么益处？因为生产者可以直接将他们的产品销售给当地社区的消费者，他们可以减少运输成本与产品的损失。消费者可以以较低的价格购买所需。

再者，当地的消费者对于当地农产品的外观不会太过苛求。生产者也能与当地消费者直接接触与沟通。因此，生产者能够收到消费者的回馈，然后生产出当地消费者喜欢的食物。

单词补充　♪ MP3 08-09

* **The Local Food Production Local Consumption Model** ph 当地食物生产当地消费模式
* **fresh** [frɛʃ] a 新鲜的
* **local market** ph 当地市场
* **directly** [dəˋrɛktlɪ] ad 直接地
* **transportation** [͵trænspɚˋteʃən] n 运输
* **demand** [dɪˋmænd] n / v 要求
* **produce** [prəˋdjus] n 农产品 v 生产
* **feedback** [ˋfid͵bæk] n 回馈意见
* **receive** [rɪˋsiv] v 收到

QUIZ!

我们来小测试一下，请填写下列空格，看你了解及学到多少。

What are the benefits of the Local Food Production Local Consumption Model? Producers can sell their products _____ to consumers in local community, meanwhile, consumers can easily enjoy the fresh _____.

_____ 模式有什么益处？生产者可以 _____ 将他们的产品销售给当地社区的消费者，同时消费者可以轻易地享用新鲜 _____。

Lesson 9
一起采买食材,下厨吧!

学习重点 1	准备采购前,不可不知的会话
学习重点 2	找篇食谱,洗手做羹汤
学习重点 3	知道异国美食的英语说法
学习重点 4	和食物相关的英语惯用语

Unit 1 采购杂货

在国外生活或旅游都会去采购杂货，我们来看几个相关对话。

 采购前

对话情境   ♪ MP3 09-01

A: Hi, Sam. I am going grocery shopping*. There's a sale going on.*
B: Really? Are there any good bargains?
A: There's a big discount* on rice, eggs, and milk. Can I get you anything?*
B: Yes, please buy me two bottles of ❶ whole milk*.

A：嗨，山姆。我要去采购杂货，现在在打折。
B：真的吗？有没有什么好折扣？
A：米、鸡蛋和牛奶都打折。要我帮你买什么吗？
B：是的，请帮我买两瓶全脂牛奶。

 寻找品项

对话情境   ♪ MP3 09-02

A: Excuse me. I'm looking for macaroni*. Where can I find it?
B: It is in Aisle* 1. You can go to the end* of this aisle and turn right. Pass two other aisles, and you will get to Aisle 1.
A: Thank you. I will check there.
B: You are welcome. Is there anything else that I can help you with?
A: No, thank you. I'm still looking around. ⟶ 等于 I'm still browsing.

A：不好意思。我在找通心粉。哪里可以找到。
B：在 1 号通道。你可以走到这个通道底，向右转。经过两个其他通道，就会到 1 号通道。
A：谢谢。我会到那找。
B：不客气。还有什么可以帮你的吗？
A：不，谢谢你。我还在逛。

单词补充   ♪ MP3 09-03

★ go grocery shopping ph. 采购杂货
  → go + v + ing 的例子还有：go window shopping 纯逛街 / go biking 去骑车 / go swimming 去游泳
★ There's a big sale going on. 大减价（可以用在任何采购场合）
★ there's a big discount on 大减价
★ macaroni [ˌmækəˈroni] n. 通心粉
  → 意大利面有各种形状；像是 farfalline 蝴蝶面

牛奶的分类有：
whole milk 全脂牛奶
2% milk 含 2% 脂肪牛奶
fat-free milk (skim milk) 脱脂牛奶
lactose-free milk 不含乳糖牛奶
flavored milk 加味奶
banana milk 香蕉牛奶

Lesson 9

 对话情境 ♪ MP3 09-04

A: How can I help you?
B: I bought the wrong type of flour this morning, and can you return* it?
A: Yes, please show me your receipt*❷.
B: Here it is.
A: Thanks. Here is your money.
B: Thank you.
A: You're welcome.

A：需要我为您服务吗？
B：我早上买错面粉了，我能退货吗？
A：是的，请给我您的收据。
B：在这。
A：谢谢。这是您的钱。
B：谢谢。
A：不客气。

 对话情境 ♪ MP3 09-05

A: How are you doing today?*
B: Fine, and thank you.
A: Paper or plastic?* Do you have our membership card?❸
B: Plastic, please, and no.
A: That's $35. Here's your change* and receipt. Do you want to have your receipt in the bag?
B: Yes, please.
A: You have a nice day.
B: The same to you. Thanks.
A: Thank you. Bye.

A：您今天好吗？
B：好，谢谢。
A：纸袋或塑料袋？您有我们的会员卡吗？
B：塑料袋，没有会员卡。
A：总共 35 元。这是找您的钱和收据。您要把收据放进袋子里吗？
B：是的。
A：祝您有美好的一天。
B：您也是。谢谢。
A：谢谢，再见。

实用句型

单词补充 ♪ MP3 09-06

★ return [rɪˋtɝn] ❶ 退还
★ receipt [rɪˋsit] ❶ 收据
★ How are you doing today? 您好吗？
（= How are you today？）
★ Paper or plastic? 纸袋或塑料袋？
★ change [tʃendʒ] ❶ 找回的钱
★ coupon [ˋkupɑn] ❶ 优惠券

❶ Please buy me 数词 + 量词 of _____ .
   请帮我买 _____ 的 _____ 。

❷ Please show me your _____ .
   请出示您的 _____ 。

❸ Do you have our _____ ?
   您有我们的 _____ 吗？

93

Unit 2 洗手做羹汤

Macaroni Cheese 起司通心粉是经典的美式意大利面，小朋友都很喜欢，我们来看看英语的起司通心粉食谱（recipe），顺便来学习与烹饪有关的英语。我们的食谱参考来源由名厨 Jamie Oliver 所提供。

Ingredients（食材）

sea salt（海盐）
freshly ground black pepper
（新鲜研磨黑胡椒）
45 g butter（45 克奶油）
3 tablespoons of flour（三茶匙面粉）
10 cloves of garlic（10 瓣蒜）
1 litre semi-skimmed milk
（1 升半脱脂牛奶）
600 g dried macaroni（600 克干通心粉）
8 tomatoes（8 颗番茄）
150 g Cheddar cheese（150 克巧达起司）
100 g Parmesan cheese（100 克帕马森起司）
olive oil（橄榄油）

Procedure（步骤）

❶ Boil the salted water*. Melt* the butter over a low heat* and add the flour into the pan*. Turn the heat up to medium and keep stirring*. Add all the sliced* garlic. Keep cooking and stirring until the garlic is done nicely.

将加盐的水煮沸。在平底锅内，小火熔奶油，并且加入面粉。再将火调至中火，持续搅拌。加入切好的大蒜。烹煮与搅拌，直到大蒜炒香为止。

❷ Slowly pour* in the milk a little at a time*. Bring the mixture* to the boil and continue stirring. After having your sauce* ready, you should preheat* your oven* to 220ºC.

每次少量慢慢加入牛奶。再把烹煮好的食材放入锅内，继续搅拌。准备好酱汁后，将烤箱以 220ºC 预热。

❸ Add Macaroni to the boiling salted water and cook. Meanwhile, chop* the tomatoes and season* them well with salt and pepper. Drain* the pasta, add it immediately to the sauce, and stir in your cheeses and chopped tomatoes.

把通心粉加入煮沸的盐水中煮。同时切番茄并且以盐和胡椒调好味。滤干通心粉，马上加入酱汁，加入起司与切好的番茄，搅拌。

❹ After seasoning everything, bake it for 30 minutes in the oven until it is done.

在调好所有味道后，在烤箱内烤 30 分钟，直到烤熟为止。

94

语法教室

❶ 分词构句

表示时间

Having finishing her homework, she felt exhausted.
= When she finished her homework, she felt exhausted.
完成功课后，她感到筋疲力尽。

表示原因

Being late for the class, he was locked outside the classroom.
= As he was late for the class, he was locked outside the classroom.
因为上课迟了，他被锁在教室外。

表示条件

Going out during the Chinese New Year, you will spend more time on the traffic.
If you go out during the Chinese New Year holiday, you will spend more time on the traffic.
如果你在中国农历新年假期外出，你会花更多时间在交通上。

表示让步

Promising to visit her, I still think I should spend more time on my work.
Although I promised to go to visit her, I still think I should spend more time on my work.
虽然答应去看她，我还是认为我应该多花点时间在工作上。

单词补充 ♪ MP3 09-07

- ★ the salted water ph 加了盐的水
- ★ melt [mɛlt] v 熔化
- ★ over a low heat ph 小火
- ★ pan [pæn] n 平底锅
- ★ stir [stɜ] v 搅拌
- ★ sliced [slaɪst] a 切片的
- ★ pour [pɔr] v 倒入
- ★ a little at a time 每次一点点
- ★ mixture ['mɪkstʃə] n 混合物
- ★ sauce [sɔs] n 酱料
- ★ preheat [pri'hit] v 预热
- ★ oven ['ʌvən] n 烤箱
- ★ chop [tʃɑp] v 切
- ★ season ['sizn] v 调味
- ★ drain [dren] v 滤干

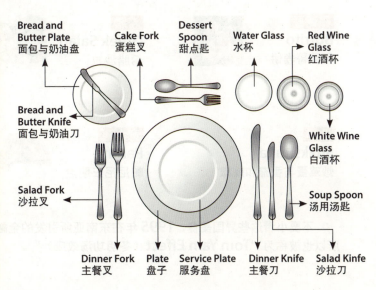

Bread and Butter Plate 面包与奶油盘
Cake Fork 蛋糕叉
Dessert Spoon 甜点匙
Water Glass 水杯
Red Wine Glass 红酒杯
Bread and Butter Knife 面包与奶油刀
White Wine Glass 白酒杯
Salad Fork 沙拉叉
Soup Spoon 汤用汤匙
Dinner Fork 主餐叉
Plate 盘子
Service Plate 服务盘
Dinner Knife 主餐刀
Salad Kinfe 沙拉刀

Unit 3 异国美食

到了国外，当然要尝尝地道的异国美食，有哪些知名的异国美食是我们必须知道的呢？

世界各国 sausage / wurst 香肠
世界各国 French fries / chip / pommes 薯条

苏格兰
Haggis
羊肉香肠

法国
Baguette
法国面包

俄罗斯
Pirozhki
炸面包

西班牙
Paella
西班牙海鲜饭

德国
Pretzel
椒盐脆饼

日本
Nigiri
握寿司

韩国
Bibimbap
韩式拌饭

墨西哥
Taco
墨西哥玉米饼

中东
Doener Kebab
沙威玛

越南 菲律宾
Balut
鸭仔蛋

墨西哥
Burrito
墨西哥卷饼

希腊
Greek Salad
希腊沙拉

新加坡
Bak Kut The
肉骨茶

北非
Shakshuka
炒鸡蛋与番茄和辣椒

意大利
Panini
帕尼尼三明治

泰国
Tom Yam
冬阴功汤

不要小看这些异国美食，1995年在东南亚所引发的金融危机，因为最先发生在泰国，所以也被称为"Tom Yam Effect（冬阴功汤效应）"。

接下来，我们先看看相关的单词，然后利用几个介绍的句型，好好地用英语来介绍长沙的夜市美食。

实用单词 ♪ MP3 09-08

碗糕 Bowl Rice Cake
车轮饼 Wheel Pies
鸡排 Chicken Fillet*
咸酥鸡 Taiwanese Fried Chicken
蚵仔面 Oyster Vermicelli*
蚵仔煎 Oyster Omelet
肉圆 Pork Balls
药炖排骨 Ribs Stewed in Chinese Herb Medicine
糖葫芦 Candied* Fruit
炸地瓜球 Fried Sweet Potato Balls
臭豆腐 Stincky Tofu

实用句型

❶ The _____ cannot be overstated.
它的 _____ 再怎么强调也不为过。

❷ "_____" is synonymous* with Chinese Night Market Food.
"_____" 就是中国夜市美食代表。

▶ 利用这几个句型，我们来介绍一下夜市美食 Stinky Tofu（臭豆腐）。

When you visit any night market in Changsha, you cannot miss the chance to taste Stinky Tofu because it represents the spirit of Changsha night-market street food.

You can choose steamed*, grilled*, or deep fried* Stinky Tofu. "Eating with sweet and sour pickled cabbage* will help to relieve* the greasiness*," goes the Changsha saying.

The popularity of Stinky Tofu cannot be overstated. Sticky Tofu is a common dish for Changsha. It's the one dish we truly can't live without.

你到访任何长沙的夜市时，不能错过尝尝臭豆腐的机会，因为它等于是长沙夜市美食的代表。
你可以选择吃清蒸、烧烤或炸的臭豆腐。俗语说："跟着酸甜的泡菜吃可以解油腻。"
臭豆腐的受欢迎程度再怎么强调也不为过。它是我们必吃的美食。

单词补充 ♪ MP3 09-09

* **fillet** [fɪlɪt] n 里脊肉片
* **vermicelli** [ˌvɝməˈsɛlɪ] n 意大利细面条
* **candied** [ˈkændɪd] a 糖煮的
* **synonymous** [sɪˈnɑnəməs] a 同义的
* **ordinary** [ˈɔrdnˌɛrɪ] a 平常的
* **steamed** [stimd] a 蒸的
* **grilled** [ɡrɪld] a 烤的
* **fried** [fraɪd] a 油炸的
* **cabbage** [ˈkæbɪdʒ] n 高丽菜
* **relieve** [rɪˈliv] v 缓解
* **greasiness** [ˈɡrizɪnɪs] n 油腻

Unit 4 英语中与食物有关的惯用表达

许多语言都有与食物有关的惯用表达用语，英语也不例外，先举出如下两个例子：

An acquired taste 需要时间慢慢习惯的人或事物
She can be said as **an acquired taste**. As you get to know her, you will like her.
她可以说是一开始不受欢迎的人。你了解她之后，就会喜欢她了。

What's cooking? 怎么了？
= What's happening?

接下来，我们再依据食物的类别来看看有哪些例子吧！

水果 ♪ MP3 09-10

 the apple of one's eye 挚爱
Rita is **the apple of my eye**. 瑞塔是我的挚爱。
apple-pie order 井然有序
Everything is in **apple-pie order** after we cleaned the house.
我们清扫房子后，所有事物都井然有序。
An apple a day keeps the doctor away. 一天一个苹果，医生远离我。

 to go bananas 为之疯狂
When the super star appears, all fans **go bananas**.
当那位超级巨星出现时，所有的粉丝都为之疯狂。

浆果 **to be as brown as a berry** 晒黑
After summer vacation, all kids **were as brown as a berry**.
暑假过后，所有孩子的皮肤都晒黑了。

樱桃 **to have another bite at the cherry** 再有一次机会
He failed the exam, but he can **have another bite at the cherry** next year.
他考试没通过，但是明年可以再试一次。

柠檬 **to buy a lemon** 买了一部烂车
Sam told me he **bought a lemon**. 山姆跟我说他买了一辆烂车。

蔬菜 ♪ MP3 09-11

黄瓜 **to be as cool as a cucumber** 非常冷静
During the earthquake, he stayed as cool as a cucumber.
地震时，他很冷静。

洋葱 **to know your onions** 精通
If you want to be an expert, you need to know your onions in the field.
如果你要成为专家，你必须精通此领域。

豆子 **to spill the beans** 走漏消息
Don't spill the beans; we intend to give her a big surprise.
不要走漏消息；我们要给她一个大惊喜。

to be full of beans 精力无限
He is full of beans. 他有用不完的精力。

坚果 **to use a sledgehammer to crack a nut** 杀鸡用牛刀
Don't use a sledgehammer to crack a nut. 杀鸡焉用牛刀。

马铃薯 **a couch potato** 成天看电视的人
On weekends, he becomes a couch potato. 在周末，他成天看电视。

a hot potato 棘手的事
This is a hot potato. 这很棘手。

面包 ♪ MP3 09-12

面包 **bread and butter** 主要收入来源
Translating is my bread and butter. 翻译是我的主要收入来源。

to have a bun in the oven 怀孕
Congratulations! Sam told me you have a bun in the oven.
恭喜！山姆告诉我你怀孕了。

奶油 **to butter somebody up** 奉承
Tom really knows how to butter her up. 汤姆真的知道如何奉承她。

be a butterfingers 笨手笨脚
I am a butterfingers. 我笨手笨脚。

蛋糕 **a piece of cake** 小事一桩
It's a piece of cake.

a share of the cake 分一杯羹
The market is huge, and everyone wants to have <u>a share of the cake</u>. 市场很大，大家都想分一杯羹。

甜点

to have a finger in every pie 事事参与
She <u>has a finger in every pie</u>. 她好管闲事。

奶蛋 ♪ MP3 09-13

起司

chalk and cheese 截然不同
They are like <u>chalk and cheese</u>. 他们截然不同。

a big cheese 大人物
He is <u>a big cheese</u>. 他是位大人物。

蛋

to put all your eggs in one basket 孤注一掷
Do diverse your investment, and do not <u>put all your eggs in one basket</u>. 要分散你的投资，别孤注一掷。

牛奶 Cry over spilt milk. 覆水难收。

鱼、肉 ♪ MP3 09-14

鱼

like a fish out of water 浑身不自在
At the party, I felt <u>like a fish out of water</u>. 在宴会中，我浑身不自在。

something is fishy 很可疑
I smelled <u>something is fishy</u>. 我觉得很可疑。

培根

to bring home the bacon 负责养家糊口的人
John needs <u>to bring home the bacon</u>. 约翰必须负责养家糊口。

饮品 ♪ MP3 09-15

汤

in the soup 有麻烦
They are <u>in the soup</u> now since they have not finished their work.
工作没做完，他们现在有麻烦了。

茶

cup of tea 菜、欣赏的对象
He is not my <u>cup of tea</u>. 他不是我的菜。

Lesson 10
去国外开开眼界吧!

学习重点 1	找到想享受的国外旅游行程
学习重点 2	看懂国外观光景点的相关资料
学习重点 3	在国外网站上订机票
学习重点 4	预订想住的饭店

旅游的类型

每个人旅游时都有不同的目的，在全球化的时代，英语成为旅游中最常使用的语言，在这个单元中，我们要学习旅游英语。首先要知道的是旅游分成哪些类型。

- **The Group Tour** 团体旅游
- **The Weekend Break** 周末假期
- **The Package Holiday** 套餐假期
- **The Caravan Road Trip** 篷车旅游
- **The RV Road Trip** 休闲居住车旅游
- **Long Term Slow Travel** 长期慢游
- **Visiting Friends or Relatives** 拜访亲友
- **Business Travel** 商务旅游
- **The Gap Year** 空档年
  → 是指花一两年的时间到海外短期工作或是旅行，欧洲许多年轻人会在高中毕业后实施空档年，思考上大学后要修读的科系。
- **Event Travel** 节事旅游
  → 为了某个活动所进行的旅行，例如 **2016** 年到巴西看奥运。

▶ 我们可以利用 5 个 wh 和 1 个 h 来开始旅游对话。

When was your last trip?
你的上一次旅游是在什么时候？

Who did you travel with?
你跟谁一起去？

What was your destination?
你的目的地是哪？

Where did you stay?
你住哪里？

Why did you visit that destination?
为什么到那个目的地去？

How did you travel there?
你如何抵达那里的？

Lesson 10

对话情境
🎵 MP3 10-01

A: Rita, when was your last trip and where did you go?
B: In winter vacation*, I went to Australia.
A: Awesome, who did you travel* with?
B: I traveled with my auntie.
A: Where did you stay?
B: We stayed with my autie's friend, Serene, in Sydney.
A: How did you get there? Did you take the direct flight* to Sydney?
B: No, I flied from Kaohsiung and then transited* in Hong Kong before arriving at my destination*, Sydney.

A: 瑞塔，你上一次旅游是什么时候？你去了哪里？
B: 寒假时，我去了澳大利亚。
A: 太棒了，你跟谁去的？
B: 我跟我姑姑去的。
A: 你们住哪？
B: 我们住在我姑姑在悉尼的朋友瑟琳家里。
A: 你怎么去澳大利亚的？你们乘坐直达班机吗？
B: 没有，我从高雄出发，在香港转机，才抵达我的目的地悉尼。

接下来，利用 5WH + 1H 的问题，把刚刚的对话内容写成一篇简单的旅游记事。

In my last trip, I went to Australia. As usual, I traveled with my auntie because she teaches in the university, and both of us have summer and winter vacations. We went to visit friends in Sydney and stayed with my auntie's friend, Serene.

For more convenience*, we flied from Kaohsiung and <u>transited</u> in Hong Kong before arriving at our destination, Sydney. Otherwise, we had to take Taiwan High Speed Rail to go to Taoyuan or spend the whole* day waiting for our <u>connecting flights</u>*, and it would take more time.

我上一次旅行去了澳大利亚。跟往常一样，我跟我姑姑去旅行，因为她在大学教书，我们都有寒暑假。我们去拜访在悉尼的朋友，住在我姑姑的朋友瑟琳家。

为了方便，我们从高雄出发，在香港转机，才抵达我们的目的地悉尼。否则，我们必须搭高铁到桃园花一整天等待转机，那会花更多时间。

单词补充
🎵 MP3 10-02

- ★ winter vacation ph 寒假
- ★ travel ['trævl] v 旅行
- ★ direct flight ph 直飞航班
- ★ transit ['trænsɪt] n / v 转机
- ★ destination [ˌdɛstə'neʃən] n 目的地
- ★ for more convenience ph 为了方便
- ★ whole [hol] a 全部的
- ★ connecting flight ph 转接班机

Unit 2 规划行程

接下来要来规划行程了，通过以下的对话，可以让我们更加了解行程规划的所有经过。

对话情境

♪ MP3 10-03

A: Where do you plan to go for your next holiday, Rita?
B: We plan to visit the U.S. this summer.
A: The U.S. is a huge country, and which part of the U.S. do you plan to go to?
B: The northwestern* states, Oregon and Washington.
A: The green pocket. Do you prefer the beach or the mountains?
B: It's a tough choice. I would say I like both.
A: Well, you are in the right region*, and there you can enjoy both beach and mountains or you can join a package tour.
B: Thank you for the advice.

A: 瑞塔，你下次打算去哪度假？
B: 我们计划今年夏天去美国。
A: 美国很大，你计划去美国的哪部分？
B: 西北部的州，奥勒冈和华盛顿。
A: 绿带州。你喜欢海边还是山区？
B: 很难的选择。两个我都喜欢。
A: 嗯，你去对了地方，你可以乐山与乐水或者你可以参加套餐行程。
B: 谢谢你的建议。

瑞塔听了建议之后，上网查看套餐行程。她只需要在 **Google** 上打关键字 **package tour**（旅游套餐）、**Oregon**（奥勒冈）、**Washington State**（华盛顿州），就会出现相关网站消息。

关键信息有以下一些：

Date	日期
Prices	价格
Explore* Vacations	搜寻假期
Company Profile	公司档案
Request Brochure*	索取手册
View Special Offers	查看特别优惠
Find Travel Agents	找寻旅行社

瑞塔键入计划旅游的日期，以不同价格去寻找适合的旅游套餐，她也查看网站上的特别优惠。另外，电脑上会弹出以下信息：

We're here to answer any questions you may have about us and help you find what you're looking for. Just fill out the information below* and our expert will be in touch with you shortly. If there is something we can help you with right away, simply call us.

我们在此回答您想知道关于我们的任何相关问题，并且协助您寻找您想要的。您只需填妥下方信息，我们的专家会尽快与您联系。如果想立即得到帮助，请拨打电话给我们。

决定好要预订旅游套餐后，依照网站指示有四个步骤：

单词补充 ♪ MP3 10-04

* northwestern [ˌnɔrθˈwɛstɚn] ⓐ 西北部的
* region [ˈridʒən] ⓝ 地区
* enlarge [ɪnˈlɑrdʒ] ⓥ 扩大、放大
* explore [ɪkˈsplor] ⓥ 探索
* brochure [broˈʃʊr] ⓝ 小册子
* below [bɪˈloʊ] ⓐⓓ 在下面
* reserve [rɪˈzɝv] ⓥ 预订
* inclusive [ɪnˈklusɪv] ⓐ 包含的

Step 1 Step 1: Click "Reserve* Now."
步骤 1：按一下"现在预约"。必须选择 **Vacation Start Date**（假期开始日期）与 **Return Date**（返回日期）。

Step 2 Step 2: "Vacation Planner."
步骤 2："假期规划师"必须提供旅游参与者的姓名、人数与年龄及欲前往地区。

Step 3 Step 3: "Inclusive* Option."
步骤 3：为包含餐点及保险等选项。

Step 4 Step 4: Make Reservation.
步骤 4：预约。

在步骤 4 必须使用信用卡或网上付款工具付款，如果要使用信用卡付款，必须提供 **Name of Card Holder**（持卡人姓名）、**Expiration Date**（有效日期）、**Credit Card Number**（信用卡卡号）及 **Security Code**（卡片背后三码的安全码）。付款后会告知您，付款已完成，并且 **Confirmation Information**（确认信息）会寄到你在 **Billing Contact Information**（账单联络信息）中提供的联络方式（通过邮件或手机短信）。

即使已经在线付款了，旅游出发时还是要查看一下您收到的付款确认信函或简讯与您附有照片的身份证明文件，像护照或驾照。

Unit 3 订机票

现在有非常多的方式可以订机票，我们分别来学习如何使用电话或柜台、网站和手机 app 来购买机票。

通过电话或柜台购买机票

对话情境

♪ MP3 10-05

A: I would like to book a flight.

B: I can help you with that. What is your destination?

A: My final destination is Portland, Oregon, U.S..

B: What date will you be traveling?

A: I would like to make a reservation* for July 18th. And I want to fly out of* Kaohsiung International Airport.

B: Then you will need to fly to Hong Kong first, and catch the flight to San Francisco before boarding* on your connecting flight to Portland, Oregon.

A: That works for me.

B: Would you prefer a morning or an afternoon flight?

A: I would like to have the morning flight.

B: Well, I have you booked on the morning flight on July 18th and you will arrive in Portland, Oregon, U.S. on the same day. Is there anything else that I can help you?

A: No, that's it. Thanks.

B: Thank you and bye bye.

A: 我要订机票。

B: 我可以帮您订票。请问您的目的地是哪里？

A: 我的目的地是美国俄勒冈州的波特兰市。

B: 您要出发的日期是哪一天？

A: 我想订 7 月 18 日的票。从高雄国际机场出发。

B: 您必须先飞到香港，然后再到旧金山转机前往俄勒冈波特兰。

A: 可以。

B: 您要搭乘早上还是下午的班机？

A: 早上的班机。

B: 好，我已经帮您订了 7 月 18 日早上的班机，您会在同一天抵达美国波特兰。还有什么我可以帮忙的吗？

A: 没有。谢谢。

B: 谢谢，再见。

在网站上订购机票

在网络上购买机票的程序与我们之前所提到的购买旅游套餐行程差不多,不过在购买机票时,各个网站对于付款与退费及更改套餐会有不同的规定,以下为两个相关范例。

Dear Passengers,

In order to avoid cases of credit card fraud*, we kindly ask you to provide the credit card originally used when asked by an airline employee during registration.

In order to rebook or refund previously purchased online tickets, it is required to* directly contact the airline via telephone or email. Please bear in mind* that it is mandatory* that you provide the airline scanned copies of your passport, and the face side* of credit card used to purchase the ticket.

亲爱的乘客,
　　为了避免信用卡诈骗,我们请您在报到时,当航空公司职员在提出登记要求时,提供信用卡。
　　为了重新订票或退回之前购买线上机票款项,您必须直接通过电话或电子邮件联系航空公司。请记得您必须提供给航空公司您的护照复印件以及您用来购买机票的信用卡正面复印件。

　　Attention! Online ticket return is made in accordance with* fare rules and is available only for tickets purchased on our website. Online tickets may be returned only if they are original and not used. We shall process the refund within ten working days from the date the ticket was returned and registered for refund. We shall not be liable for* the time taken to clear funds through banks. Online tickets may be refunded in any currency*. Before processing your ticket return online, please read our Refund Policy.

　　请注意!线上机票退款依据机票费用规定,并且只适用在网上所售的机票。线上机票只能在提出正本并且未使用的情况下,予以退费。我们会在机票退回并且登记退款之日起的十个工作日内处理退款。我们不负责银行计算费用的时间。线上机票可以以任何货币进行退款。在您申请线上退款前,请详阅我们的退款政策。

语法教室

only if 的用法

Only if 其实是条件式说法,必须前者先成立后者才成立。
Only if I finish my work, I will go home.
我要做完工作才回家。(没完成工作就不回家)
The venue will not open on Sundays only if there is an event.
这个设施星期天不会开放,除非有活动。(没活动就不开放)

Be liable to 负责及有义务的用法：

The supplier is liable to pay the VAT during a transaction.
供应商有义务在交易时支付增值税。

If you drink and drive, you can be liable to great penalties.
如果你酒驾，你会受到重罚。

使用 App 购买机票

使用 App 购买机票，除了方便外，还可以让你掌握第一手的信息！我们来看下列短文。

Do you have any idea to start searching cheap flight deals? Please trust us that our App is a good place to start[1]. You can use this App on either Android or iOS devices. You can browse flights from almost all airlines including budget airlines. You can also compare over a thousand flight rates. With the simple filter feature and a few seconds, you can get yourself a desirable flight deal.

你知道要从哪里开始搜便宜机票吗？相信我们，我们的 App 是你搜机票的好地方。你可以在 Android 或 iOS 系统上使用这个 App。你可以看到几乎所有的航空公司票价，包括廉价航空机票在内。你可以比较近千个航班的票价。只需要使用简单的过滤器功能以及几秒钟，你就可以找到你想要购买的机票。

单词补充 🎵 MP3 10-06

* to make a reservation ph 预约
* to fly out of ph 从……出发
* board [bord] v 登机
* credit card fraud ph 信用卡诈骗
* be required to ph 必须
* to bear in mind ph 请记得
* mandatory ['mændətɔrɪ] a 有义务的、必需的
* the face side ph 正面
* in accordance with ph 依据
* be liable for ph 负责
* currency ['kɜrənsi] n 货币

实用句型

_____ is a good place to start.
_____ 是一个可以开始的好地方。

For start-ups, the Internet is a good place to start.
对新创公司而言，网络是一个可以开始的好地方。

For bloggers, this website is a good place to start.
对博主而言，这个网站是一个可以开始的好地方。

Unit 4 住宿的类型

订好机票后，总不能露宿街头，所以接下来要搞定的就是住宿。住宿有哪些选择、需要懂哪些英语？我们一起来学习。住宿的分类不少，没有人确切知道到底有多少种，我们就先学习常看到的分类词汇。

Hotel 饭店、酒店，有 1~5 星级分级
- boutique hotel 精品酒店
- business hotel 商务酒店
- capsule hotel 胶囊酒店

Resort 度假村
- chalet 小木屋
- lodge 小屋
- ski lodge 滑雪小屋
- hunting lodge 狩猎小屋
- treehouse 树屋
- igloo 冰屋

Villa 别墅

Tent 帐篷

Apartment 公寓

▶ 每个住宿地都会有自己的名称，可以上网看照片及浏览之前入住的顾客的评论意见，许多旅游网站都会提供类似信息。例如：

We stayed two nights in June at this lovely pension. With its friendly * staff, delightful * breakfast, comfortable old-style * room, and convenient * location, we loved this place and highly recommend * it.

我们在 6 月时在这个可爱的民宿住了两个晚上。民宿友善的员工、美味早餐、舒适的古典房间和方便的地点让我们爱上了这个地方并且强力推荐。

The lift looked like the suicide scene *. The carpet on the floor was dirty and coated with * dust. The door of our room was not secure *. There is hair on our bed sheets *. "Can it really be that bad? *" you may ask. Trust me; yes, it can.

电梯看起来像是自杀现场。地板的地毯很脏，满是灰尘。我们的房门一点也不安全。我们的床单上有毛发。你可能会问："真的有这么糟吗？"相信我，真的这么糟。

Are you prepared to❶ sleep in beds made of* snow and ice? If you are, you can be the customer of an ice hotel.

Even though the temperature of an ice hotel is below zero Celsius*, it is still warmer than outside. Furthermore, staying at an ice hotel for a night will cost a fortune*, at the price of hundred or even thousand US dollars.

Another benefit to❷ stay at an ice hotel is that you can enjoy ice sculptures* at the lobby. You also have food prepared "cold" for the special circumstance*. You can sit on ice bench* to enjoy your meals.

Don't worry about❸ getting too cold. When you are sleeping, you will be given furs*, blankets*, and sleeping bags* to keep you warm.

你是否已经准备好睡在雪和冰制成的床上？如果你准备好了，你就可以成为冰旅馆的顾客。
虽然冰旅馆的气温低于零度，但还是比外面温暖。再者，在冰旅馆住一晚可不便宜，数百元或甚至一千元美金一晚。
另一住在冰旅馆的好处是你可以观赏大厅的冰雕。你也可以享用为此特别状况准备的"冷食"。你可以坐在冰凳上享用餐点。
不要担心你会太冷。你睡觉时会有皮毛、毯子和睡袋让你保暖。

实用句型

❶ Are you prepared to _____?
你准备好 _____ 了吗？

❷ Another benefit to _____.
_____ 的另一个好处。

❸ Don't worry about _____.
别担心 _____。

其他住宿

- hostel 青年旅馆、平价旅馆
- Bed and Breakfast 民宿
- guesthouse 招待所、民宿
- camp 帐篷营地饭店
- ice hotel 冰旅馆
- farmhouse 农舍
- motel 汽车旅馆
- cottage 旅馆
- inn 旅馆
- chateau 古堡
- pension 民宿
- castle 城堡

单词补充 🎵 MP3 10-07

- friendly ['frɛndlɪ] a 友善的
- delightful [dɪ'laɪtfəl] a 美味的
- old-style [old staɪl] a 舒适的古典房间
- convenient [kən'vinjənt] a 便利的
- highly recommend ph 强力推荐
- suicide scene ph 自杀现场
- to be coated with ph 布满
- secure [sɪ'kjʊr] a 安全的
- bed sheet ph 床单
- Can it really be that bad? 真的有那么糟吗？
- to be made of ph 由……所制成
- Celsius ['sɛlsɪəs] a 摄氏的
- to cost a fortune ph 花掉一笔钱
- ice sculpture ph 冰雕
- circumstance ['sɜkəmstæns] n 状况
- ice bench ph 冰凳
- fur [fɝ] n 皮毛
- blanket ['blæŋkɪt] n 毯子
- sleeping bag ph 睡袋

Lesson 11
收拾行李，出发旅行去！

学习重点 1 ｜ 准备去国外旅行
学习重点 2 ｜ 到国外的机场报到登机
学习重点 3 ｜ 用英语和饭店人员沟通

Unit 1 收拾行李，准备出发

传奇人物 Ibn Battuta（伊木•白图泰）告诉我们：Traveling – it leaves you speechless, then turns you into a storyteller.（旅行先是让你无言，然后再把你变成一位说故事者。）所以我们做好所有预约后，最重要的当然是出发去旅行，一起走吧！

首先，我们要先准备一份 checklist，"checklist" 单词的中文意思为"清单"，在出发旅行之前，我们就需要为自己列一张旅行用的 checklist，以免有遗漏，耽误了行程，以下就来看看在你的旅行清单上要列出哪些项目。

Traveling Checklist 旅行清单

- ☐ **Traveling documents (passport, visa, international driver's license, insurance documents, and tickets)**
  旅行证件（护照、签证、国际驾照、保险文件与票券）
- ☐ **Flight information (airline and airport information, flight times)**
  航班信息（航空公司及机场信息、航班时间）
- ☐ **Luggage (packing and weight)** 行李（打包及重量）
- ☐ **Currencies and credit cards**（现金货币及信用卡）
- ☐ **Destination information (weather, news)** 目的地信息（天气、新闻）

▶ 首先，要先知道护照与签证有什么不同？通过下面一篇英语文章的阅读，我们来了解护照与签证的不同与重要性。

Like National Identity Cards* we are holding, passport is required when we travel abroad for identification purposes*. Stamps are also given when passport bearers* enter and leave their own countries.

On the other hand, visa is issued by a destination country government that foreign travelers would like to visit temporarily*. Visa normally states the duration of stay, territory* for visitors to enter, the entry dates, or the number of visits authorized*.

The big difference between visa and passport is they are issued by different governments and with different purposes: passport issued by the national government for its citizens* and visa issued by the government of destination country for foreign visitors. There are various* types of passports and visas, such as ordinary passport and diplomatic* passport as well as tourist visa, transit* visa, and business visa.

Lesson 11

就像我们持有的身份证，我们出国旅游时需要护照来辨识身份。护照持有人在进入与离开自己国家时，护照上都会盖章。

另一方面，签证由外国旅客想短暂到访的目的地国家政府所颁发。签证通常会说明停留期间、访客进入的领土范围、进入日期或所许可的到访次数。

签证与护照的最大不同点在于由不同的政府所发：护照由本国政府发给其公民，而签证则由旅游目的地政府发给外国访客。护照与签证各有不同类型，例如，一般护照与外交护照，以及旅游签证、过境签证与商务签证。

单词补充　♪MP3 11-01

★ **National Identity Card** ph. 国民身份证
★ **for identification purpose** ph. 证明身份用
★ **passport bearer** ph. 护照持有人
★ **temporarily** [ˈtɛmpəˈrɛrəlɪ] adv. 短暂地
★ **territory** [ˈtɛrətorɪ] n. 领土
★ **authorized** [ˈɔθəˌraɪzd] a. 经授权的
★ **citizen** [ˈsɪtəzn̩] n. 公民
★ **various** [ˈvɛrɪəs] a. 不同的
★ **diplomatic** [ˌdɪpləˈmætɪk] a. 外交的
★ **transit** [ˈtrænsɪt] n./v. 通过、过境

▶ 利用刚刚学到的单词，来进行造句学习：

- You should bring your **National Identity Card** with you when you stay late at a pub.
  在酒吧中待得比较晚时，你必须带着身份证。

- This document is used **for identification purpose**.
  这份文件用来做辨识用。

- All U.S. **passport bearers** are required to sign their names on the signature page.
  所有持有美国护照者都必须在签名页签名。

- Please print the name of **credit card holder**.
  请正楷书写信用卡持有人姓名。
  → **bearer** 跟 **holder** 都是持有人的意思，例如：**credit card holder** 信用卡持有人

- The train was **temporarily** suspended due to an accident.
  因为意外的原因，火车暂时停驶。

- This distributor has been only **authorized** to undertake the sales of products in this **territory**.
  该经销商只被授予在此领土内销售的产品。

- The company provides cost effective **transit** for its customers.
  那家公司为顾客提供具成本效益的转运。

对话情境　　打包行李　　♪ MP3 11-02

A: I heard you are going to the US for vacation next month. Are you packed?*

B: Not yet.* I'd better go pack for the trip. Especially, this time, I'll travel with* my niece. Documents, credit cards, money, clothes, shoes, and toiletries…The list can go on two days.*

A: I happen to* have some tips for you to pack quickly and easily.

B: I need them desperately.*

A: First, you need to let your niece to pack with you. Let her get involved and help you. She will then share the responsibility for packing and get excited* for the trip.

B: That is such a good idea. She will have more fun from packing.

A: Use coupons or buy travel size* items that will not take up too much space* and be thrown away* at the end of your trip.

B: That's helpful since I will travel with a kid, we have to pack many things.

A: The last tip is to buy what you need when you get there. Usually, it's convenient to shop in the US. Oh, you also need empty* plastic bags to keep dirty clothes in.

B: Yes, these bags can be useful.

A：我听说你下星期要去美国度假，你打包好了吗？

B：还没。我最好得打包了。特别是这一次我要跟我侄女一起去旅行。文件、信用卡、钱、衣服、鞋子和盥洗用品……要打包的东西说三天三夜也说不完。

A：我刚好有几个诀窍可以让你更快速与轻松地打包。

B：我真的很需要。

A：首先，你要让你的侄女一起来打包。让她参与，并且帮助你。她就可以分担责任并且对旅行充满期待。

B：这是个好主意。她会从打包中获得乐趣。

A：用折价券或购买旅行装用品，这样不会占太多空间，旅行结束前，你还可以把这些东西丢掉。

B：这很有帮助，我跟小孩一起旅行，我们必须打包许多东西。

A：最后一个就是到当地再买你需要的东西，通常在美国购物很方便。你也需要一些空塑料袋来装脏衣服。

B：是的，这些袋子很好用。

★注意上面对话中英语套色的内容，非常实用！

接下来，我们通过对话中出现的重要单词，进一步学习。

- **Are you all packed?** 你打好包了吗？
  或是 Are you all packed? Are you done packing?

- **Not yet.** 还没。
  A : Have you finished your work? 你的工作完成了吗？
  B : Not Yet. 还没。

- **The list can go on two days.** 三天三夜都说不完。
  Every day, we use a lot of petroleum products: socks, buttons, underwear, body lotion, and Aspirin. The list can go on two days.
  每天我们都使用许多石化产品：袜子、纽扣、内衣、乳液与阿司匹林。三天三夜都说不完。

- **to travel with**… 跟谁去旅行
  This summer I will travel to the US with Rita. 这个夏天我要跟瑞塔去美国。

- **I happen to**… 我刚好……
  I happen to have the schedule with me. 我刚好带着时间表。

- **desperately** 急迫地
  I need them desperately. 我非常需要。
  He is desperately looking for a job. 他很急迫地在找工作。

- **to get excited** 感到振奋、很期待
  We only live once; we should get excited about life.
  人生只有一次；我们应该对生命感到振奋。

- **to have fun from** 从……获得乐趣
  It is easy to have fun from work. 要从工作中获得乐趣很简单。

- **travel size** 旅行装
  Travel size products give you more convenience.
  旅行装产品给你更多便利。

- **to take up too much space** 占太多空间
  This furniture takes up too much space of the living room.
  这件家具占用太多客厅空间。
  ※**to take up too much time** 占用太多时间
  Our conversation took up too much of my time.
  我们的谈话占用我太多的时间。

- **to throw away** 丢掉
  This can be used again, so do not throw it away.
  这个还可以再用，所以不要丢掉。

- **empty** 空的
  During the Chinese New Year, streets in Taipei were empty.
  在农历新年时，台北的街道空空荡荡的。

一篇好的文章不一定要写得生动活泼，但一定要有完整的起承转合架构。在这里，我们来学习英语写作中常用的转折、接续用语。

根据文章中上下句的逻辑关系，找出最恰当的转折用语，转折用语的功用如润滑剂一样，目的是告知下一句的性质与立场，一般可以分成改变语气、接续、结论……

on the other hand 另一方面

He is busy * at work; on the other hand, he would like to spend more time with his family.
他忙于工作，另一方面，他想多花点时间在家人身上。

on the contrary 反之

We shall have gone straight *; on the contrary, he made a right * turn.
我们应该直走，相反地，他右转了。

rather than 而不

I would go to bed rather than go out for a drink.
我宁可上床睡觉，也不想外出饮酒。

yet 然而

He had been working very hard *, yet he was not promoted *.
他很努力地工作，然而未获得升迁。

nevertheless 然而

She was angry at him; nevertheless, she still went out with him.
她对他生气，然而还是跟他出去了。

会话补充 Conversation　　♪MP3 11-03

A: Do you want to go shopping * with me?
B: No thanks. I'm so tired. I would like to stay at home rather than go out for shopping.
A: Okay. Take a rest *.

A: Why are you doing this?
B: What are you talking about?
A: You were angry at Eric; nevertheless, you went out with him last night.

A: 你想要和我去逛街吗？
B: 不想，谢谢。我好累，我宁可待在家，也不想出去逛街。
A: 好吧，好好休息。

A: 你为什么要这样做？
B: 你在说什么？
A: 你对艾瑞克生气，然而昨天晚上还是跟他出去了。

单词补充　♪MP3 11-04

* busy [ˈbɪzɪ] a 忙碌的
* straight [stret] a 直的
* right [raɪt] a 右边的
* hard [hɑrd] a 努力的
* promote [prəˈmot] v 升迁
* go shopping  逛街
* rest [rɛst] n/v 休息

利用转折、接续的用语，可以让文章的连贯性更强，且阅读起来更为流畅，流畅的文章能够帮助读者更容易抓到文章重点。

as long as 只要

As long as you finish your work, you can go for a vacation this weekend.
只要你完成工作，你这个周末就可以去度假。

as a result 因此

They were not ready yet. **As a result**, the test will be put off*.
他们还未准备好。因此，考试将延期。

apart from the fact that 即使

Apart from the fact that global economy is slowing down, consumers do not react very sensitively* to price rises.
即使全球经济衰退，消费者也并没有对物价上涨有过度的反应。

consequently 因此

Now you have no time for bodily* exercise, and **consequently**, you will find time for illness* later.
现在你没时间运动，因此，之后你就得腾出时间来生病。

furthermore 再者

Furthermore, we need to conduct* more studies to understand the relationships* between adults and children.
再者，我们需要进行更多研究，以了解成人与儿童之间的关系。

suddenly 突然地

Suddenly, everything changed.
突然间，一切改变了。

now that 既然

Now that he was retired*, he moved away from the city.
既然他已经退休了，他就搬离了市区。

单词补充 ♪ MP3 11-05
- ★ put off ph. 推迟、拖延
- ★ sensitively ['sɛnsətɪvlɪ] adv. 神经过敏地
- ★ bodily ['bɑdɪlɪ] a. 身体的
- ★ illness ['ɪlnɪs] n. 疾病
- ★ conduct [kən'dʌkt] v. 带领、处理
- ★ relationship [rɪ'leʃənʃɪp] n. 关系
- ★ retired [rɪ'taɪrd] a. 退休的

大家常分不清楚旅游警报（**travel alerts**）和旅游警告（**travel warnings**）的差别，下一篇文章告诉你其中的差别。

A travel alert is issued for short-term events including strikes*, demonstrations, outbreak of infectious diseases* or threats of terrorist attacks* for travelers to think what they should plan before traveling to the country. When these causes disappear, the travel alert will be cancelled.

Meanwhile, a travel warning is issued for travelers to decide whether they will still travel to the country. Reasons to issue a travel warning include unstable political situation, civil war*, intense* crime or violence, or frequent terrorist attacks. A travel warning aims to stop travelers to go to the country, and some traveling warnings may remain effective for several years.

A five-colored coded system of traveling alerts has been used to announce the threat levels. The severe, high, significant, general, and low risks are respectively shown in red, orange, yellow, blue, and green colors. Recently, several national governments issued yellow travel alerts to travelers who plan to go to Brazil and Australia due to the outbreak of yellow fever and elevated threat of terrorist attack.

旅游警报针对短期事件发出，包括罢工、示威、疾病的爆发或恐怖袭击，提醒旅客思考出发到该国之前的规划。原因消除时，就会取消旅游警报。

同时，旅游警告会发出，让旅客决定是否仍然前往该国。发给旅游警示的原因包括不稳定的政治情况、内战、激烈犯罪、暴力或频繁的恐怖袭击。旅游警告的目的是制止旅客前往该国，有些旅游警告持续好几年。

五个颜色制度的旅游警告被用来公告威胁程度。严重、高度、重大、一般及低度风险程度分别以红色、橘色、黄色、蓝色和绿色来标示。最近，数个国家政府就针对黄热病的爆发及升高的恐怖袭击威胁对欲前往巴西与澳洲的旅客发出黄色旅游警告。

▶ 这篇文章的重要单词与例句如下： ♪ MP3 11-06

strike [straɪk] n 罢工	Taxi drivers in Toronto planned to stage a **strike** this weekend. 多伦多的出租车司机酝酿在本周末罢工。
outbreak of infectious diseases ph 传染病暴发	The **outbreak of infectious diseases** raised the question about the preparedness of the public health system. 传染病的爆发引发公共卫生系统是否完善的问题。
terrorist attack ph 恐怖袭击	ISIS claimed the responsibility for **terrorist attacks** in several countries. "伊斯兰国"声称在几个国家发动了恐怖袭击。
civil war ph 内战	He studied the causes of the American **Civil War** fighting between 1861 and 1865. 他研究 1861 年至 1865 年的美国内战。
intense [ɪnˈtɛns] a 激烈的	The injury caused **intense** pain. 受伤造成剧烈疼痛。

Unit 2 机场报到

出发旅行后，我们很快就会来到机场报到登机，来看看我们需要用到哪些英语会话。

对话情境 在航空公司的登机报到柜台

♪ MP3 11-07

A: Good day. Where are you flying to today?
B: San Francisco.
A: May I have your passport, please?
B: Here you are.
A: Are you checking in any bags?
B: How many bags can I check in?
A: Two.
B: I'll check in these two pieces, and I will have the small one to take on the airplane as a carry-on*.
A: Alright, please place your bags on the scale.
B: My stopover* in the US is Los Angles. Will I need to pick up my luggage there?
A: No, the baggage inspection* is conducted at the destination port, and your luggage will go directly to San Francisco. Would you prefer an aisle seat or a window seat?
B: Aisle seat, please.
A: Here are your boarding passes – your flight leaves from gate 26, and it will begin boarding at 11:20. Your seat number is 24C. Please leave after your bags have been checked by the X-ray machine.

A：您好，请问今天飞往哪里？
B：旧金山。
A：请把护照给我？
B：在这里。
A：您有任何要托运的行李吗？
B：我能托运几件？
A：两件
B：我要托运两件，小的我要带上机，作为登机行李。
A：好的，请把行李放在磅秤上。
B：我到美国的第一站是洛杉矶，我需要在那里领行李吗？
A：不，行李检查会在目的地机场，您的行李会直接挂到旧金山。您想靠走道还是靠窗坐？
B：靠走道。
A：您的登机牌在此，您的登机门在 26 号，11:20 将开始登机。您的机位号码是 24C。请在 X 光机检查完您的行李后再离开。

119

基于安全的原因，地勤人员也会在你报到登机时问你下列问题：

- **Did you pack your bags yourself?**
  您的行李是自己打包的吗？
- **Has your luggage been in your possession* at all times?**
  您是否一直都看管着您的行李？
- **Are you carrying any firearms* or flammable* materials?**
  您是否携带了任何枪支或易燃物品？

安检（**security check**）时会使用的英语如下：

- **Please lay your bags flat on the conveyor* belt, and use the bins for small objects.**
  请把袋子平放在输送带上，并且使用盘子放置小东西。
- **Please step back. Empty anything in your pockets: keys, cell phone, and change.** 请往后站。清空口袋：锁匙、手机和零钱。

登机牌信息

拿到 Boarding Pass（登机牌）后，你必须注意的重要信息如下：
Name of Passenger
（乘客姓名）
Flight Number（航班号码）
Date（日期）
Boarding Time（登机时间）
Boarding Gate（登机门）
Seat Number（座位号码）
Scheduled Departure Time
（预定起飞时间）

另外，看过登机牌信息、通过安检后，也必须注意听广播：

- **Singapore Airlines Flight Number SQ2 to San Francisco is now boarding*. Please have your passport and boarding pass with you.**
  新加坡航空公司 SQ2 前往旧金山的航班现在开始登机。请准备好护照及登机证。
- **We would now like to invite all passengers to board.** 我们现在邀请所有乘客登机。
- **This is the final boarding call for Singapore Airlines Flight Number SQ2 to San Francisco.**
  这是新加坡航空公司 SQ2 前往旧金山班机的最后登机通知。

单词补充 MP3 11-08

- **carry-on** [ˈkærɪˌɑn] a 可随身携带的
- **stopover** [ˈstɑpˌovɚ] n 中途停留
- **inspection** [ɪnˈspɛkʃən] n 检查
- **possession** [pəˈzɛʃən] n 所有物
- **firearms** [ˈfaɪrˌɑrmz] n 枪支
- **flammable** [ˈflæməbl] a 易燃的
- **conveyor** [kənˈveɚ] n 运输装置（＝ conveyer）
- **board** [bord] v 登机

对话情境 — 机上点餐 MP3 11-09

A: Ma'am, what would you like for lunch, sandwich or pasta?
B: Pasta, please.
A: Would you like to have anything to drink?
B: Just water with ice.
A: Here you go.
B: Thank you.

A：女士，您午餐要用三明治，还是意大利面？
B：请给我意大利面。
A：您要喝点什么吗？
B：只要水加冰块。
A：请用。
B：谢谢。

Unit 3 饭店入住

对话情境　登记住房　　♪ MP3 11-10

A : Good evening! Welcome to Metropolis Hotel.

B : Good evening! My name is Sally Wu.

A : Alright, Ms. Wu. Let me call up your reservation*. Hmm…I cannot find your booking record. Did you book directly from us or did you use a hotel reservation system?

B : I used a hotel reservation system. Here's the reservation number.

A : Thank you. We will upgrade* you to a bigger room since we ran out of single rooms.

B : Do I need to pay extra?

A : Certainly, there will be no extra charge to you.

B : Thank you.

A : You're welcome.

B : How can I use❶ wireless* connection?

A : The access code* is your room number, 608. If you have any questions, just let us know. Please fill out the form for me.

B : Sure.

A : This is your room key, and please take the elevator* on the right to go to the eighth floor.❷ When you go out of the elevator, please turn right and go down to the hallway to get to your room.

A：晚上好！欢迎来到大都会饭店。

B：晚上好！我的名字是吴莎莉。

A：好的，吴女士。让我找一下您的订房记录。嗯……我找不到您的订房记录。您是直接通过我们订的房还是使用饭店预约系统呢？

B：我使用的饭店订房系统。这是订房号码。

A：谢谢。因为我们没有单人房了，我们将为您升级到较大的房间。

B：我需要额外付费吗？

A：当然不需要。

B：谢谢。

A：不客气。

B：我要如何使用无线网络？

A：上网密码是您的房间号码，608，如果您有任何问题，请告诉我们。请帮我填写这张表格。

B：好。

A：这是您的房间钥匙，请右转，坐电梯到八楼。您走出电梯后，请右转，然后走到底，就到您的房间了。

121

B : Thank you.
A : Here is the voucher* for your breakfast③. Breakfast will be served between 7:00 and 10:00 at the Plaza Café. Have a nice stay.

B：谢谢您。
A：这是您的餐券。早餐在 7:00 到 10:00 之间由广场咖啡馆供应。祝您住宿愉快。

实用句型 MP3 11-11

单词补充
* reservation [ˌrɛzɚˈveʃən] n 预定
* upgrade [ˈʌpɡred] v 升级
* wireless [ˈwaɪrlɪs] a 无线的
* access code n 登入密码
* elevator [ˈɛləˌvetɚ] n 电梯（手扶梯是 escalator）
* voucher [ˈvaʊtʃɚ] n 餐券

❶ How can I use _____?
我要如何使用 _____？

❷ Please take the elevator on the _____ to go to _____ .
请搭 _____ 的电梯去 _____。

❸ Here is the voucher for your _____ .
这是您的 _____ 票券。

对话情境 客房点餐服务 MP3 11-12

A : How can I help you?
B : Hi, I am calling from 608. I would like to order something for dinner.
A : Right, Ms. Wu.
B : I would like to have garden salad and seafood pasta.
A : Would you like to have something to drink?
B : Yes, do you serve wine?
A : No, for alcoholic drinks, you can go directly to the bar at the lobby.
B : Ok, then I would have Coke Zero. How long would that take?
A : Just a few minutes, madam.
B : That sounds great. Thank you.

A：有什么可以为您服务的吗？
B：嗨，这里是 608 号房。我想要晚餐服务。
A：好的，吴小姐。
B：我要田园沙拉与海鲜意大利面。
A：您需要饮料吗？
B：可以点酒吗？
A：不可以，您可以直接到一楼酒吧享用酒精饮料。
B：好的，那我要零卡可乐。大概需要多久的时间？
A：女士，只需要几分钟。
B：太好了，谢谢您。

对话情境 退房　　　♪ MP3 11-13

A : Are you ready to check out?
B : Yes.
A : Can I have your room key and what room were you in?
B : Here you go, and my room is 608.
A : How was your stay? Were you satisfied with everything?
B : I really enjoyed my stay here.
A : I am glad that you had good experience when staying with us. Would you be putting this on your credit card?
B : Yes.
A : Ok, and the total amount comes to US$173.99 with tax. Please sign here.
B : Alright.
A : Here's your receipt and you are now all set.

A：您准备好要退房了吗？
B：是的。
A：可以给我您的房间钥匙吗？您住几号房？
B：在这里，我住608号房。
A：您喜欢您的住房吗？一切都满意吗？
B：我真的喜欢在这里的住房。
A：我很高兴您住房愉快。是否要以信用卡付款？
B：是的。
A：好的，含税总共173.99美元。请在此签名。
B：好。
A：这是您的收据，您已经完成退房了。

▶ 如果要表示对某人或某事不满意的话，要怎么说呢？
… not satisfy 人 = 人 is not satisfied with…
……令某人不满意

That move did not **satisfy** him.
= He **was not satisfied with** that move.
他对那个举动不满意。

She cannot **satisfy** her husband.
= Her husband **is not satisfied with** her.
她无法令她丈夫满意。

写作小教室

我们利用之前学到的单词,写一篇关于 travel size products(旅行用品)的介绍文章吧!画线的词汇便是刚刚学过的内容。

<u>Are you all packed</u> for your trip? <u>Not yet!</u> Here are some tips for you.

→ **写作技巧**
使用问题作为开场,引起注意。

你打包好准备出发去旅行了吗?还没!这里有几个诀窍跟你分享。

Packing can be very tiring and slow, and <u>the list can go on and on.</u> You, however, can <u>have more fun from packing</u> and make you <u>get more excited</u> for the trip.

→ **写作技巧**
先陈述打包的问题,再举正面范例,改变对打包的观感。

打包是很累、又很慢的工作,要打包的东西三天三夜都说不完。但是,打包可以给你更多乐趣,让你对旅行更期待。

Travel size products, for example, can <u>give you more convenience</u>. They are not only small in size but also cheap in price. With coupons, you can even get them free. They will not <u>take much space</u>. Furthermore, you can <u>throw them away at the end of your trip.</u>

→ **写作技巧**
切入主题,讨论优点。

例如旅行套装产品,可以给你更多的便利。他们不仅尺寸小,价格也便宜。有折价券时,你还可以免费获得。不会占太多空间。再者,旅行结束时,可以丢掉。

会话补充 Conversation ♪ MP3 11-14

A: Do you have any suggestions for Katie's birthday gift?
B: Certainly. I know she's a big fan of Hello Kitty.
A: That's a good idea.
B: I happen to know she's looking for a handbag.
A: Really? That's so helpful.
B: You know her style. She's cute.
A: Yes, then I should buy her a pink Hello Kitty handbag then.
B: Good choice.

A: 你可以给我有关凯蒂生日礼物的建议吗?
B: 当然。我知道她很喜欢凯蒂猫。
A: 真是好主意。
B: 我碰巧知道她想买个手提包。
A: 真的?这帮了我大忙。
B: 你知道她的风格。她很可爱。
A: 是的,我应该给她买个粉红色的凯蒂猫包。
B: 好选择。

Lesson 12
趁着购物季，大肆采买吧!

学习重点 1 | 到国外的实体店大采购
学习重点 2 | 和外国店员进行对话
学习重点 3 | 用英语询价与议价

Unit 1 实体店铺种类

"超低折扣、物美价廉、全年无休、快速到货、免运费"这些让人忍不住掏出信用卡的词到底要如何使用英语来说呢？很简单，他们分别是：

- 超低折扣 super discount
- 物美价廉 good value, good bargain
- 全年无休 open all year round
- 快速到货 fast shipping quick delivery
- 免运费 free shipping

没错，接下来的两堂课，我们就来学习如何使用英语来购物。今天的购物其实是实体店铺与网络购物平台的战争。我们就来看看购物的例子。

我们先就实体店铺的种类来学习相关英语词汇与例句：

- shopping center / shopping mall ph 购物中心
  Convenience is always the first concern* for people who go shopping at shopping malls.
  便利一直是人们到购物中心购物的第一考量。

- department store ph 百货公司
  Department stores frequently offer monthly sales.
  百货公司通常会每个月提供折扣。

- boutique store ph 精品商店
  Boutique stores often update their unique inventory*.
  精品商店常更新他们独特的库存。

- specialty store ph 专卖店
  Specialty stores only sell items related to a specific brand.
  专卖店只销售特定品牌的相关物品。

- outlet store / factory store ph 畅货商店 / 工厂直营商店
  At outlet stores, some products are never sold at the retail* level.
  在畅货商店，有些产品从未在零售商店销售过。

- wholesale store ph 批发商店
  At wholesale stores, we usually buy products at low prices.
  在批发商店，我们通常可以以低价购买产品。

- retail store ph 零售商店
  Reducing the price is a strategy* seldom used by retailer stores.
  降低价格是零售商店较少使用的策略。

- chain store ph 连锁商店
  Sometimes, not all chain stores charge customers the same price.
  有时候，并不是所有连锁店都对顾客收取同样的价格。

- franchise store ph 加盟店
  Franchise stores are used to distribute* goods while the investment* is relatively lower.
  加盟店可以用来分销货物，但是投资相对比较低。

Lesson 12

语法教室

❶ 频率副词，放在 be 动词与助动词之后，一般动词之前

always 总是
He always has his coffee in the morning. 他总是在早上喝咖啡。

never 绝不
If he never gave up*, he would be a rich man now.
如果他当初不放弃，他现在应该是有钱人了。

seldom 很少
They seldom talk to each other. 他们彼此之间很少讲话。

usually 通常
My mom usually goes swimming in the morning. 我妈通常早上去游泳。

frequently 常常
These are frequently asked questions. 这些是常见问题。

sometimes 有时候
Sometimes we go out* for movies. 有时候我们会出去看电影。

often 经常
Rita and Amber often play together. 瑞塔和安柏经常在一起玩。

ever 从来、至今
Have you ever been to Australia? 你去过澳大利亚吗？

❷ 表示次数的副词短语

once for a while 偶尔
I visit him in Taipei once for a while.
我偶尔会去台北看他。

now and then 有时
Now and then, we discuss* our projects.
有时我们会讨论专案。

once again 再次
Once again, I would like to remind you about the importance* of this issue.
我要再次提醒你这个问题的重要性。

单词补充 🎵 MP3 12-01

★ concern [kənˈsɜn] n 关心的事
★ inventory [ˈɪnvəntorɪ] n 存货
★ retail [ˈritel] n 零售；零售的
★ strategy [ˈstrætədʒɪ] n 战略
★ distribute [dɪˈstrɪbjut] v 分发
★ investment [ɪnˈvɛstmənt] n 投资
★ give up ph 放弃
★ go out ph 外出
★ discuss [dɪˈskʌs] v 讨论
★ importance [ɪmˈpɔrtns] n 重要性

Unit 2 购物时对话

对话情境　　　♪ MP3 12-02

A : How are you doing today?
B : I am doing fine, and thank you.
A : Great! What can I help you with? Are you looking for something in particular*?
B : I am looking for a shirt.
A : How about this? It's on sale, and you will enjoy a 20% discount.
B : Do you have it in a smaller size?❶
A : Sorry, we are out of smaller sizes in blue color. What other colors do you like?
B : I will take the white one. May I try it on?❷
A : The fitting rooms* are over there.

A：您今天好吗？
B：我很好，谢谢。
A：太好了！有我能够服务的地方吗？您是否在寻找特定的东西？
B：我在找衬衫。
A：这件如何？正在打折，您可以享八折优惠。
B：有小一点的尺寸吗？
A：不好意思，蓝色的没有小尺寸的了。别的颜色可以吗？
B：我拿白色的好了。可以试穿吗？
A：试衣间在那。

在国外，店里的销售人员会在顾客一上门时，就笑眯眯地打招呼说：Hi!（嗨！）How are you？/ How are you doing today?（您好！）

而顾客只需要回应：Fine, thank you.（很好，谢谢。）或 Fine, and you?（很好，你呢？）

听到了你的回应后，店里的销售人员会进一步提供协助，并且说：What can I help you?（有我能够服务的地方吗？）或 Are you looking for something in particular?（您是否在寻找特定的东西？）

这时候你就可以告知你在找的东西。
I am looking for a shirt. 我在找衬衫。

接着店员就会告知你要找的东西的地点在哪里或者直接给你看你要找的东西。
How about this? 这件如何？
It's on sale, and you will enjoy a 20% discount.
这件正在打折，您可以享八折优惠。

sale 打折的英语思维逻辑跟中文相反，所以"今天您可以享有七折的购物优惠"，英语可得说：You will receive a 30% off / discount for your shopping today.

实用句型

❶ Do you have it in a smaller size? 有小一点的尺寸吗？
若想要问其他颜色时，可说 Have you got this in another color?
（有其他颜色吗？）

❷ May I try this one? 我可以试穿吗？
= Where may I try this on? 我可以在哪里试穿？

对话情境 🎵 MP3 12-03

A: How did it fit?
B: Good, and I will take it.
A: Great! I can help you at the checkout counter*.

A：合身吗？
B：不错，我要买。
A：太好了！我到柜台帮您结账。

对话情境 🎵 MP3 12-04

A: How did it fit?
B: It does not fit me. It's too big.

A：合身吗？
B：不适合我，太大了。

在试衣间内常会用到的英语会话还有：
- How much is it? 多少钱？
- It's too long. 太长。
- It's too expensive. 太贵。
- I don't like it. It's not what I want.
  我不喜欢。这不是我要的。

接下来，就可以综合上面所学的内容，和店员进行对话了！

会话补充 Conversation 🎵 MP3 12-05

A: Are you looking for something in particular?
B: Do you have a dress for a party?
A: How about this? It's on sale, and you will enjoy a 25% discount.
B: Where may I try this on?
A: The fitting rooms are over there.
A: How did it fit?
B: I don't like it. I look like a sausage. It's not what I want.

A：您在找特定的商品吗？
B：你们有派对穿的连衣裙吗？
A：这件如何？正在打折，您可以享有七五折优惠。
B：我可以在哪里试穿？
A：试衣间在那里。
A：合身吗？
B：我不喜欢。我看起来像香肠。这不是我要的。

129

对话情境　　　♪ MP3 12-06

A: Should I gift wrap* it?
B: No. That's for myself.
A: Do you want anything else?
B: No, that's all for today.
A: That comes to US$29.99 with a 20% discount. Do you need a bag?
B: No. Do you take traveler's check?
A: I'm sorry. We do not take traveler's checks.
B: Ok, I will pay cash*.
A: Do you happen to have any change*?
B: No.
A: Here is your change. US$71.01. Thank you for shopping with us today, and enjoy your new shirt. Bye bye.
B: Bye bye.

A: 您要礼物包装吗?
B: 不用，我自己穿。
A: 您还需要别的东西吗?
B: 不，今天都买齐了。
A: 打八折后，29.99美元。您需要袋子吗?
B: 不需要。您收旅行支票吗?
A: 抱歉。我们不收旅行支票。
B: 好，我付现金。
A: 您有零钱吗?
B: 没有。
A: 这是找您的钱。71.01美元。谢谢您今天在我们店里购物，希望您喜欢新衬衫。再见。
B: 再见。

在柜台结账时，柜台人员都会有礼貌地询问您购买的物品是要自用，还是要送人:
Should I gift wrap it? 您要礼物包装吗?
你可以回答: **No. That's for myself.**（不用，我自己要用的。）或 **Yes, please.**（是的，请帮我包装。）

在国外购物，袋子通常需要额外付费，如果柜台人员问你: **Do you need a bag?**（您需要个袋子吗?）你回答 **Yes, please.**（是的，我需要。）柜台人员就会接着说:
That comes 30 cents. Is it ok for you?（一个30美分，您可以接受吗?）

付款的时候，询问付款方式的句型则为:
Do you take traveler's check? 您收旅行支票吗?
Do you take credit card? 您收信用卡吗?

如果你提供的现金金额过大，店家希望你使用较小金额付款时，就会询问: **Do you happen to have any change?**（您有零钱吗?）

单词补充　　♪ MP3 12-07

★ **particular** [pəˈtɪkjələ] a 特殊的
★ **fitting room** n 试衣间
★ **checkout counter** n 结账柜台
★ **gift wrap** [gɪft ræp] v 包 n 礼物包装
★ **cash** [kæʃ] n 现金
★ **change** [tʃendʒ] n 零钱

Unit 3 折扣与议价

折扣一般很吸引消费者，英语中与折扣有关的句型有哪些呢？　🎵 MP3 12-08

询问折扣

A: Is this on sale?
B: There's a discount of 30% off the original price.
A: How much discount can I get?
B: You can get a 10% discount if you buy two package courses*.

A：这有打折吗？
B：打七折。
A：我能获得多少折扣？
B：如果您购买两个套装课程的话，就可以获得10%的折扣。

促销活动

A: What's the sales promotion* program available* now?
B: You can get one free* smart phone when you buy one from us.

A：现在有什么促销计划？
B：只要向我们购买一个智能手机，您就可以免费获得另一个。

▶ 买一送一 英语叫作 "Buy one, get one free" 或 "Buy one, get one"。

折价券

- With the coupons, you are able to enjoy 5% off for in-store* shopping. 利用折价券，您可以享有在店内购物九五折。
- Our reward* cards help your save your money on your shopping. 我们的回馈卡能让您在购物时省钱。

调降售价

Prices are reduced* to sell. According to news report, Apple has cut the price of the 6s and 6s Plus by up to 16% off the original price point.
售价已下降。新闻报道指出，Apple 已经将 6s 与 6s plus 的原价调降了16%。

活动优惠

Every weekend, we offer a special brunch* set deal.
每个周末，我们都提供特别的早午餐优惠。

单词补充 🎵 MP3 12-09

* **package courses** n 套装课程
* **promotion** [prə'moʃən] n 促销
* **available** [ə'veləbl] a 可获得的
* **free** [fri] a 免费的
* **in-store** [ɪn'stɔr] a 库存的
* **reward** [rɪ'wɔrd] n / v 报偿
* **reduced** [rɪ'djust] a 降低的
* **brunch** [brʌntʃ] n 早午餐

131

砍价是交易中的一部分，在许多国家，人们习惯砍价，商家也很习惯把价钱提高让顾客来进行砍价，以下是用英语来砍价的情境。

接下来学几句在询价的时候很重要的句子：
❶ Give me a discount. 给我打个折吧。
❷ Can I get a discount? 可以算便宜点吗？
❸ It's a little overpriced. 这价钱有点贵。
❹ It's too expensive. 这个太贵了。
❺ I'd buy this if it were cheaper. 再便宜一点我就买。
❻ Lower the price and I'll consider it.
价钱再低一点我才会考虑。

对话情境

🎵 MP3 12-10

A: How much are you asking for this antique clock?
B: It's yours for 100 Euros.
A: That's a bit high.
B: Since you are my first customer today, how about 80 Euros?
A: That sounds about right.
B: Done.

A：这个古董钟卖多少钱？
B：卖你100欧元。
A：有点贵。
B：因为你是我今天第一位顾客，就卖你80欧元如何？
A：听起来不错。
B：成交。

对话情境

🎵 MP3 12-11

A: I like everything about it except the price.
B: But I already gave you a 10% discount
A: That's still a bit high. I've seen this cheaper in other places.
B: All right, how about 75 dollars?
A: I'd take it for 70 dollars. That's all I have.
B: Okay, you should know it's a really good deal.
A: Thanks a lot.

A：这件东西除了价钱外，其他的我都很喜欢。
B：但我已经给你九折了。
A：还是有点贵。我在别家店看到过更便宜的。
B：好吧，75美元如何？
A：如果70美元我就买。这是我所有的钱。
B：好吧，你知道这是个真的不错的交易。
A：谢谢。

数字练习

不管是折扣还是砍价，会说和能听懂才是关键，我们来看看英语中的数字有哪些差异。

❶ 单数、复数

一个名词叫"单数"，两个以上就叫"复数"。

少
- A boy is playing at the park. 一个男孩在公园玩。
- Two boys are playing at the park. 两个男孩在公园玩。
- Several boys are playing at the park. = A few boys are playing at the park. 几个男孩在公园玩。

多
- Many boys are playing at the park. 许多男孩在公园玩。

❷ 可以用来修饰不可数名词的量词

little 很少；几乎没有 Little milk is left in the glass.
杯子中几乎没有牛奶。

much 许多 Much milk is left in the glass.
杯子中还有许多牛奶。

a little 一些 A little milk is left in the glass.
杯子中还有一些牛奶。

❸ 用来排列顺序用"序数"

第 1 到第 3	第 4 到 12	第 20 至 90	第 21 之后
the first the second the third	the fourth the fifth the sixth the seventh the eighth the ninth the tenth the eleventh the twelfth	the twentieth the thirtieth the fortieth the fiftieth the sixtieth the seventieth the eightieth the ninetieth	the twenty first the twenty second the twenty third the twenty forth …

- If you are the first customer to come to our store, you will receive a free gift.
如果您是第 1 位来店里的顾客，您将可以领取一份免费的礼物。

- Their second son was named Jimmy.
他们的第 2 个儿子取名为吉米。

- They won the third place in the singing contest.
他们在歌唱比赛中赢得第 3 名。

- Pearl is the traditional symbol for the 30th wedding anniversary.
珍珠是结婚 30 周年的象征物品。

- After your 21st birthday, you are allowed to consume alcohol.
你 21 岁生日后，就可以喝酒了。

中英语数字的转换

个位数 1～9	one to nine 常搞混数字：**4** four, **5** five
十位数 10～99	ten to ninety-nine 常搞混数字：13～19 thirteen to nineteen 与 30～90 thirty to ninety；45 forty-five 与 54 fifty-four
百位数 100～999	one hundred to nine hundred and ninety nine，也可念成 nine hundred ninety nine，但 504 就一定要念成 five hundred and four
千位数 1 000～9 999	one thousand to nine thousand nine hundred and ninety nine 比较一下：1,001 one thousand and one / 1,010 one thousand and ten / 1,100 eleven hundred
万 10 000～99 999	ten thousand to ninety nine thousand nine hundred and ninety nine 比较一下：10,001 ten thousand and one / 10,010 ten thousand and ten / 10,100 ten thousand and one hundred / 11,000 eleven thousand
十万 100 000～999 999	one hundred thousand to nine hundred ninety nine thousand nine hundred and ninety nine 比较一下：100,001 one hundred thousand and one / 100,010 one hundred thousand and ten / 100,100 one hundred thousand and one hundred / 101,000 one hundred and one thousand / 110,000 one hundred and ten thousand
百万 1 000 000～ 9 999 999	one million to nine million nine hundred ninety nine thousand nine hundred ninety nine ★ 1.5 million = 150 万
千万 10 000 000～ 99 999 999	Ten million to ninety nine million nine hundred ninety nine thousand nine hundred ninety nine ★ 23.2 million = 2 320 万
亿 100 000 000～ 999 999 999	One hundred million to nine hundred ninety nine million nine hundred ninety nine thousand nine hundred ninety nine ★ 540.4 million = 5,404 亿
十亿 1 000 000 000～ 9 999 999 999	one billion to nine billion nine hundred ninety nine million nine hundred ninety nine thousand nine hundred ninety nine ★ 1.23 billon = 12.3 亿
百亿 10 000 000 000～ 99 999 999 999	ten billion to ninety nine billion ★ 22.3 billion = 223 亿
千亿 100 000 000 000～ 999 999 999 999	one hundred billion to nine hundred ninety nine billion ★ 580.2 billion = 5 802 亿
兆 1 000 000 000	trillion

Lesson 13

网络购物超方便！

- 学习重点 1 ｜ 在国外网站上购物
- 学习重点 2 ｜ 用英语询问订购内容
- 学习重点 3 ｜ 和购物有关的英语用语

Unit 1 在网络上购物

在学习完商店购物的相关英语后,接下来要介绍线上购物,首先我们先学习与网上购物有关的英语单词。要享受全年无休的线上购物,你需要懂得与线上购物相关的这些英语名词。

- **web browsing** 浏览网站
  Internet connection 网络连接 / **search engine** 搜寻引擎 / **webpage** 页面 / **link** 链环
- **new or second-hand items** 新品或二手商品
- **Add to Shopping Cart** 新增至购物车
  Checkout 结账 / **Continue Shopping** 继续购物 / **a credit or debit card** 信用卡或借记卡 / **price comparison** 比价
- **drop down list** 下拉清单
  check box 可勾选方格 / **field** 栏位 / **CAPTCHA** 随机码 / **Refresh** 更新
- **order summary** 订单摘述
  Submit 送出 / **Proceed** 处理 / **order confirmation** 订货确认单
- **contact and delivery details** 联系与送货详细资料
  post code 邮政区号

认识了以上的单词你就可以上网购物了!大家都知道,要网上购物,只需要有网络及信用卡或借记卡,然后利用搜寻引擎,登入购物网站与网页,搜寻你要的商品,比价之后,决定要购买的项目,加入购物车确认后,填写好个人联系方式、信用卡信息与送货地址,结算付费后,购物网站就会进行处理,整个线上购物程序就完成了,你就只需要等着收货就行了。

下面我们就利用以上单词来写一篇介绍网上购物的文章,我们从网上购物的流程开始。上面学过的单词,在文章中也会用符号标示。

Lesson 13

Online shopping gives us a lot of convenience because how to shop online is easy and simple. What you need first is to have the Internet connection* and your credit card* or debit card ready.

Then you need to use a search engine* to look for a particular product or brand that you are interested in. Type any new or second-hand items* to get to your desirable websites, webpages or useful links*. You can begin your price comparison* and put things you like by clicking Add to Shopping Cart*. If you are happy with your shopping, you can either go to Checkout or you can hit Continue Shopping.

After that, you are required to fill in a form of your contact and delivery details* including post code*❶. After completing all fields*, drop down lists*, check boxes*, and CAPTCHA*, you can press "Submit*" to send out your form. If you make any mistake, just refresh* your form and start it over.

Before making the payment, do remember to read order summary* carefully. When the page displays "Proceed*," your order has been sent and received. Later, you will also receive a form of order confirmation*. What you need to do then is to wait for your order to arrive at your door.

　　网上购物带给我们许多便利，因为网上购物很轻松、很简单。你只需要有网络与信用卡或借记卡就可以进行网上购物。

　　然后你必须使用搜寻引擎来寻找你感兴趣的特定产品或品牌。输入任何新的或二手物品，你就可以到你所想要到访的网站、网页或是有用的链接。你可以开始比价并且通过按一下"增至购物车"，加入你喜欢的事物。如果你对于购物满意的话，就可以前往"结账"或选择"持续购物"。

　　接着，你就必须填写你的联络与送货详细资料，包括你的邮区号在内。填妥这些栏目、下拉式选单、勾选方格与随机码后，你就可以按下"送出"将你的表格送出。如果你犯下任何错误，只需要更新表格，重新填写一次即可。

　　在付款前，要记得详细阅读订单详情。页面显示"处理"时，你的订单就已经送出并且由对方收到了。之后，你也会收到订货确认单。你现在只需要等待订单送到家门口就行了。

写作小教室

如何描述说明步骤呢？把自己当作新手，把每个步骤都想一遍。

因此，先想象自己是个网购新手，第一个步骤就是要工欲善其事，必先利其器。先准备好电脑及信用卡或借记卡。接着就是依照我们在网上购物的程序，一步一步地执行。

STEP 1 使用搜寻网站、浏览器，再输入你感兴趣的新品或二手商品

STEP 2 第二个步骤是比价……

接着再把程序交代清楚，网上购物程序的文章就完成了。

语法教室

对等相关连接词短语

both...and 两者都

She is fluent in both French and Spanish. 她的法语跟西班牙语都说得很好。

as well as 也是

There are some new as well as creative ideas in this book.
那本书有些新奇及有创意的想法。

not only...but also 不仅……而且……

Our products are made not only for children but also for the elderly at home.
我们的产品不仅适合家中小孩，也适合长辈。

either...or 或（两者之一）

Either you or John needs to attend the meeting.
你或约翰其中一个必须去开会。

neither... nor 两者皆不

He ate neither an apple nor an orange. 他没吃苹果，也没吃橘子。

对话情境   🎵 MP3 13-01

A: Where did you get the watch from?[2] It's so cool.

B: I got it from abcwatch.com.

A: Online shopping? Don't you find it dangerous?

B: No, it's secure. You can find both new and second-hand items with good bargains.

A: That sounds interesting.[3]

B: With the internet connection and your credit card or debit card ready, online shopping can be just easy and convenient.

A: Do I need to wait a long time to get my order?

B: No. Shipping is fast, and return is easy.

A: Wow, that's great. I will look at the website today.

A: 你的表在哪买的？看起来很棒。

B: 我在 abcwatch.com 买的。

A: 网上购物？你不觉得危险吗？

B: 不，网上购物很安全。你可以用低价买到全新跟二手商品。

A: 听起来很有趣。

B: 通过网络，准备好你的信用卡或借记卡，购物可以很简单及便利。

A: 我需要等很久才能拿到货物吗？

B: 不用。送货快，退货容易。

A: 哇，太好了。我今天就上网站看看。

实用句型

❶ You are required to fill in a form of _____.
你必须填写表格中的_____。

❷ Where did you get _____ from?
你在哪里买_____？

❸ That sounds _____.
听起来很_____。

单词补充   🎵 MP3 13-02

- ★ connection [kəˈnɛkʃən] n 连接
- ★ credit card ph 信用卡
- ★ search engine ph 搜寻引擎
- ★ item [ˈaɪtəm] n 物品
- ★ links [lɪŋks] n 连结
- ★ comparison [kəmˈpærəsn] n 比较
- ★ Shopping Cart ph 购物车
- ★ delivery detail ph 送货详细资料
- ★ postal code ph 邮递区号
- ★ CAPTCHA ph 随机码、验证码
- ★ submit [səbˈmɪt] v 提交
- ★ refresh [rɪˈfrɛʃ] v 更新
- ★ order summary ph 订单摘要
- ★ order confirmation ph 订购确认单

Unit 2 线上购物的电话与书信往来

上网购物不管是购买有形的货物还是无形的服务，总会有打个电话或书信往来的时候，我们来看看怎么打电话与怎么写信。

▶ **Sally**（莎莉）要为侄女瑞塔（**Rita**）打电话去博物馆登记夏令营活动。
电话中的交易最重要的是交易日期、内容、个人信息、付款资料等，如同对话中的画线词。

对话情境　　　　　　　　　　　　　♪ MP3 13-03

A : Hi, Children Museum. This is Tom. What can I help you with?

B : Hello, I am calling to register for the <u>summer camp</u>.

A : Yes, which date would you like to have for the summer camp?

B : The one starting from <u>June 27th</u>.

A : June 27th, ok! May I have your first and last name?

B : Yes, <u>Sally Wu</u>.

A : Did you register with us last year?

B : Yes, but unfortunately, there were not enough children registered, so the camp was cancelled.

A : Yes, we had it cancelled last year, and I am glad that you are still interested this year.

B : Yes, we are. I am also glad that you still kept our information.

A : You are welcome. Are you ready for the payment?

B : Yes.

A : What card is it?

B : <u>visa card</u>.

A：儿童博物馆，您好，我是汤姆，我能帮您什么呢？

B：您好，我打来报名夏令营活动。

A：好的，哪一天的夏令营活动？

B：6月27日开始的。

A：6月27日？请告知我您的姓名。

B：是的，吴莎莉。

A：您去年有报名吧？

B：是的，但是很遗憾，报名的儿童人数不够，所以夏令营取消了。

A：是的，我们去年取消了。很高兴您今年仍然感兴趣。

B：是的，我们很感兴趣，我很高兴您仍然留着我们的信息。

A：不客气。您可以付款了吗？

B：是的。

A：什么卡？

B：威士卡。

A : Does it have your name, Sally Wu, on it?
B : Yes.
A : I will take the numbers if you are ready.
B : Ok. They are 000011112222.
A : When is the expire date?
B : June, 2020.
A : Okay, we now have your payment, and I will send you the relevant information via email. Please have the forms signed and return to us.
B : I will.
A : Contact us if you have any problems. We will see Rita in June.
B : Thank you and goodbye.

A：持卡人是您的名字，吴莎莉吗？
B：是的。
A：您准备好就可以给我号码了。
B：好的。000011112222。
A：有效日期是什么时候？
B：2020年6月。
A：好的，我们收到您的付款了，我会再通过电子邮件把相关信息发给您，请把表格签好，再寄还给我们。
B：我会的。
A：如果有任何问题请联络我们。我们跟瑞塔6月见。
B：谢谢，拜拜。

▶ Sally（莎莉）在英语网站上订了间民宿，接着等待回应，在这期间房东写了封信给她。

Hi, Sally:

Welcome to Monterey! You are the best aunt we have ever seen! To be honest, we never host anyone here longer than four days. We would like to host you, but we have a couple of concerns. First of all, you don't smoke❶, do you? Second, where you are going to live here has no access to a kitchen❷, but a coffee machine, a toaster, a microwave and a refrigerator, no stove, exactly like the photos in our profile pages. Third, we only provide basic TV program❸. Are these okey for you?

Also, may we ask how old is your niece as well?❹ Thanks a lot and have a good day!

Clara and Keith

嗨，莎莉：
　　欢迎来到蒙特雷！您是我们知道的最好的姑姑！老实说，我们还没招待过住宿四天以上的客人。我们想要招待您，但是有几个考量点。首先，您不抽烟吧？其次，您要住的房间没有厨房，只有咖啡机、烤面包机、微波炉和冰箱，没有炉子，就像您在我们的资料照片中看到的一样。再次，我们只提供无线电视台节目。这样您可以接受吗？
　　另外，我们也想知道您的侄女几岁？谢谢，祝您有美好的一天。

克莱拉与凯斯

收到这样的信，如果不回复，即使在网站上付了钱，房东还是不会安心地把房子租给你，所以一定要仔细阅读信中的问题，并且回答问题。（可见两封邮件中的画线词与编号的对应）

Dear Clara & Keith,

  Thank you for the email and prompt reply, and about your concerns, we are all ok. I don't smoke❶, and last year, we were also in Monterey for Rita's summer camp. We stayed at a motel and had no access to a kitchen, either.❷ I studied in MIIS before, and I am quite familiar with the area and know where to get foods. Rita basically will stay at the camp from 9:00 to 15:30 from Monday to Friday, and the camp will provide her lunch. On weekends, we will go to some tourist spots.❸ Your place will suit our need very much. Rita is now 7.❹

  Hopefully, we will be able to stay with you, and I am sure that we will enjoy it. Thank you again for your kind consideration.

Sally

克莱拉与凯斯，你们好：

  谢谢你们的电子邮件与快速回复，关于你们提出的考量，我们都没问题。我不抽烟，去年我们也去了蒙特雷，让瑞塔参加夏令营。我们住在汽车旅馆，也没有厨房用。我在蒙特雷国际研究院读过书，对当地很熟，知道到哪买食物。瑞塔基本上星期一至五，9:00 到 15:30 都会待在夏令营，那里供中餐。假日时，我们会去旅游景点。你们的房间非常适合我们的需求。瑞塔现在七岁了。

  希望我们能够住在你们那里，我确定我们会很喜欢。再次谢谢您的贴心考虑。

莎莉

在回信中，要使用礼貌性用语，并且回复问题。

礼貌性用语

- **Thank you for the email and prompt reply.**
  谢谢您的电子邮件与即时回复。
- **Your place will suit our need very much.**
  你们的房间非常适合我们的需求。
- **Hopefully, we will be able to stay with you.** 希望我们能够住在你们那里。
- **I am sure that we will enjoy it.** 我确定我们会很喜欢。
- **Thank you again for your kind consideration.** 再次谢谢您的贴心考虑。

年份、日期、时间的英语

年
2000   Year Two Thousand
2008   Two Thousand (and) Eight, Twenty O Eight
2016   Twenty Sixteen

日
March 30 / March 30ᵗʰ
= The Thirtieth of March
3 月 30 日

时间
1:00   One O'clock
1:20   One Twenty, Twenty Minutes Past/After One
1:30   One Thirty, Half Past One
1:45   One Forty Five, A Quarter to Two

回复问题

- About your concerns, we are all ok. 你们的关注点，我们都可以接受。
- I don't smoke. 我不抽烟。
- We stayed at a motel and had no access to a kitchen, either.
  我们住在汽车旅馆，也没有厨房可以用。（主要回复点）
- Last year, we were also in Monterey for Rita's summer camp.
  去年我们也去了蒙特雷，让瑞塔参加夏令营。（次要回复点）
- I studied in MIIS before, and I am quite familiar with the area.
  我在 MIIS 念过书，对当地很熟。（次要回复点）
- The camp will provide Rita lunch. 夏令营供给瑞塔中餐。（次要回复点）

这样清楚、具有说服性的回复，当然让房东很放心，接着房东就来了这么一封信：

> Ha, you are the one that sells seashells by the sea shore. Thank you very much for the promptly responding. <u>We almost accept your request until we thought of another thing we forgot to mention. Our son is going to practice his piano seven out of the 12 days during your staying. About 40 minutes to an hour each time.</u> Besides of this we are a quiet family. Is this acceptable to both you and Rita? If this is okay, we will see you in June. Thanks a lot!
>
> **Clara and Keith**
>
> ---
>
> 哈，您说服了我们。谢谢您快速的回复。我们几乎可以接受您的要求，但是我们想到另外一件事忘了提。我儿子在您住宿的 12 天内有 7 天必须练习钢琴，每次约 40 分钟到一个小时。除此之外，我们家都很安静。这对您跟瑞塔来说可以接受吗？如果可以的话，我们 6 月见，谢谢！
>
> 克莱拉与凯斯

注意 "to sell seashells by the sea shore" 除了在音上面是有处绕口令外，也意味着在此已表明说服了房东把房子租出去。但是有诚意的房东还是要再做最后的提醒，即信中画线的部分。

回了这封电子邮件之后，网站就传来了订房已确的信息！书信往来沟通目的成功！

> No problem, and that reminds me that Rita needs to practice her piano, too. Thank you for being so considerate.
>
> **Sally**
>
> ---
>
> 没问题，这提醒了我，瑞塔也需要练习她的钢琴。谢谢你们这么贴心。
>
> 莎莉

Unit 3 与购物有关的英语惯用语

购买 buy

to buy a pig in a poke 冲动地购买
You should be careful not to buy a pig in a poke.
你要小心点，不要轻率地购买。
→ impulsive buyer / purchaser 冲动的购买者

to buy the farm 死了
He bought the farm last month. 他上个月去世了。

购买 shop

to shop someone 告发
Because she broke the law, he shopped her to the police.
因为她违法了，他就向警察告发她。

to shop around 货比三家
They are shopping around for a tablet.
他们为了买平板电脑而货比三家。

to shop till you drop 买到累瘫或破产为止
Hong Kong is a place where you will shop till you drop.
香港是个会让你逛街逛到累倒的地方。

购物 shopping

window shopping 纯逛街
I often go window shopping on weekends.
我周末时常去逛街。

shopping list 购物清单
This app helps you easily create your shopping list.
这个应用程序协助你轻松建立购物清单。

shopping spree 疯狂购物
During the annual sale of the department store, she went out on a shopping spree.
百货公司周年庆期间，她疯狂大采购。

shopping therapy 购物治疗
I have been stressed out recently, and shopping therapy may work for me.
我最近压力很大，可能可以用得上购物治疗。

to shoplift 顺手牵羊
A lot of celebrities were caught shoplifting.
有许多名人因为顺手牵羊被逮捕。

支付 pay

🎵 MP3 13-07

to pay one's way 不欠债支付自己的生活
He failed to pay his way.
他欠债了。

to pay over the odds 高出价格的购买
Since we are paying over the odds for energy, there will be the cut of electricity bill payment in April.
因为我们支付过高的能源费用，四月起电费会调降。

to pay through the nose 花很多钱
It is not wise to pay through the nose for a designer bag.
花那么多钱买这个名牌包不明智。

商店 shop

🎵 MP3 13-08

to be all over the shop 到处
They looked for the teddy bear all over the shop.
他们到处找那只泰迪熊。

to shut up shop 结束了
We should shut up shop.
我们该结束了。

to talk shop 三句不离本行
You should not talk shop at a party or you will bore others.
在宴会中不该三句不离本行，否则你会让大家觉得很无趣。

a bull in a china shop 行动鲁莽的人
Being panic, he acted like a bull in a china shop.
惊慌之余，他的行动很鲁莽。

chop shop 汽车销赃店
The police officer was accused of operating a chop shop.
这名警察被控诉经营汽车销赃店。

pop-up shop 临时的实体商店、快闪商店
This pop-up shop is set up to sell big brands.
这家快闪商店是卖名牌的。

happy shop 卖酒的商店
There always is a long line in front of the happy shop.
卖酒的商店前面总是大排长龙。

sweatshop 血汗工厂
The report on sweatshop caught a lot of attention.
这篇血汗工厂的报道引起许多人的注意。

closed shop 封闭型工会制度

In the past, you needed to be a member of a closed shop if you were doing your business.

以前如果你要做生意，必须是工会会员。

Keep your shop, and your shop will keep you

善于经营必能致富

From this billionaire, I have learned "keep your shop and your shop will keep you."

从这位亿万富翁身上，我学到"善于经营必能致富"。

to set up your shop 开店

It's easy to set up your own shop online.

在线上开设自己的商店很容易。

品牌 brand
试穿 try on

own brand 自制品牌

At this drugstore, you can find both its' own brands and well-known brands.

在这家药房，你可以找到它的自制品牌与其他知名品牌。

→ **genuine brand** 真品牌（具有品牌价值并且有让消费者认同的价值）

to try it on 唐突无理

They tried it on with the new teacher.

他们对那个新来的老师大胆无礼。

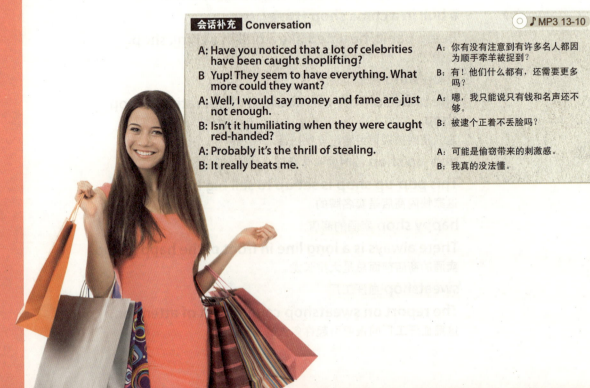

会话补充 Conversation	MP3 13-10
A: Have you noticed that a lot of celebrities have been caught shoplifting?	A：你有没有注意到有许多名人都因为顺手牵羊被捉到？
B: Yup! They seem to have everything. What more could they want?	B：有！他们什么都有，还需要更多吗？
A: Well, I would say money and fame are just not enough.	A：嗯，我只能说只有钱和名声还不够。
B: Isn't it humiliating when they were caught red-handed?	B：被逮个正着不丢脸吗？
A: Probably it's the thrill of stealing.	A：可能是偷窃带来的刺激感。
B: It really beats me.	B：我真的没法懂。

Lesson 14
一定要知道的职场英语!

学习重点 1 | 撰写英语求职信
学习重点 2 | 进行英语面试
学习重点 3 | 用英语向公司做自我介绍

Unit 1 工作内容与求职信

在全球化的今天,大家经常使用英语来沟通,不论是从事哪一行、出租车司机、商贩、店员、公司中的员工,在工作上都得说英语,我们就从工作职责要求、求职信与面试等程序开始,学习用英语来谈论工作吧!

工作职责

来看看基层人员的工作内容,基层人员的英语是 entry level,有时候也会使用 junior level,相对之下,资深人员就叫作 senior level。

Experience* / Education* / Qualification* 经验 / 教育 / 资格	0~2 years professional* experience. 0~2 年的专业经验。 With Bachelor's Degree* or equivalent*. 学士或同等学力。 The ability to communicate in English is a plus. 最好能使用英语沟通。
Skills* 技能	Knows fundamental* concepts, practices and procedures of particular field of specialization. 了解特定特殊领域的基本概念、惯例及程序。
Duties* / Tasks* 责任 / 任务	Uses established* procedures, works under immediate supervision*, and performs assigned* tasks. 在立即的监督下,使用已经建立的程序与工作惯例,执行所派给的工作。 Routine* work and instructions* are usually detailed. 工作具规律性,说明包括详细资料。
Usually Report to 报告对象	Supervisor 主管

Lesson 14

求职信

了解了以上的工作职责要求后，因为资格要求是"最好能使用英语沟通"。所以如果对这个职位感兴趣，可以写封英语的求职信应征。

Eric Lin
900-1 Dunhua East Rd.,
Taipei, 12032
Mobile phone number: 0900000000
Email: askme@gmail.com

March 22, 2016

Dear Hiring Manager,

My name is Eric Lin. I came across your job posting online. I am very interested in this job position of❶ engineer. I believe I'm the right candidate* you are looking for.

There are several reasons. I have more than two years of operation* experiences in❷ the panel making industry*. I major in❸ mechanics* and hold a Bachelor's Degree as the company requires. I have been working in the English speaking environment in a high-tech* company since I graduated from the university, and I scored 850 in TOEIC❹.

My theoretical* knowledge and practical skills in the professional field equip* me the qualification you are looking for. I researched your company and found the philosophy* of your company to have something in common with mine, striving for greatness. I am a quick learner, and I have the enthusiasm* and determination* to learn.

Please find enclosed my CV in application. Thank you very much for your time and consideration*, and I look forward to hearing from you. Should you require any additional* information, please contact me.

Respectfully Yours,

Eric Lin

尊敬的人事经理：

　　我的名字是艾瑞克·林。我在线上看到您的招聘。我对于工程师职位很感兴趣。我相信我是您在寻找的人。有几个理由。我在面板业有两年多的经验。按公司规定，我主修机械并且有学士学位。我大学毕业后，一直在讲英语的高科技公司环境中工作，我的托业成绩为 850 分。

　　我在专业领域的理论知识及实务技能让我具备了您所寻求的资历。我也对公司做了研究，发现公司理念跟我有共同点，追求伟大。我学得很快，并且我对学习有热诚与决心。

　　我的应征函中也附上了我的简历。谢谢您，期待您的回复。如果您需要任何其他信息，请与我联络。

致敬

艾瑞克·林

这是一封标准的求职信，只有一页。从结构来看，不包括信头的联系信息、称谓、日期与信尾签名，只有三段，分别为前言、主体与结尾。

联络信息

求职信在一开始就必须清楚地附上应征者的联系信息，必须包括姓名、地址、手机号码与电子邮件地址，接着还要附上日期。

称谓

求职信都是寄给负责招聘员工的人事经理的，在称谓上可以使用 Mr. / Ms. Smith 史密斯先生 / 女士。

如果不知道人事经理的姓名，可以像上述求职信范例一样，简单地称呼 Hiring Manager（人事经理）。

前言

在求职信的前言中你必须说明：

❶ 姓名。

My name is＿＿＿＿＿＿＿. 或 I am＿＿＿＿＿＿＿.

❷ 告知如何得知这个职位。

I came across your job posting online. 我从您线上的征才信息得知职缺消息。

❸ 提及你要应征的工作项目。

I am very interested in this job position of engineer. 我对工程师的职位很感兴趣。

❹ 说服对方为什么你是他们要的人。

I believe I'm the right candidate you are looking for. There are several reasons. I have more than two years of operation experiences in the panel making industry. I major in mechanics and hold a Bachler Degree as the company requires. I have been working in the English speaking environment in a high-tech company since I graduated from the university, and I scored 850 in TOEIC.

我相信我是您在寻找的人。有几个理由。我在面板业有两年多的经验。按公司规定，我主修机械并且有学士学位。我大学毕业后，一直在讲英语的高科技公司环境中工作，我的托业成绩为 850 分。

150

主体

❶ 更进一步地说明你的资历与公司所要求的极为吻合。
My theoretical knowledge and practical skills in the professional field equip me the qualification you are looking for.
我在专业领域的理论知识及实务技能让我具备了您所寻求的资历。

❷ 可以进一步地提及你对公司所做的研究与发现。
I researched your company and found the philosophy of your company to have something in common with mine, striving for greatness.
我也对公司做了研究，发现公司理念跟我有共同点，追求伟大。

❸ 在主体的结尾处以你的个人特点与优势作为小结。
I am a quick learner, and I have the enthusiasm and determination to learn.
我学得很快，并且我对学习有热诚与决心。

结尾

❶ 在结尾段落中要告知重要的信息与感谢。
Please find enclose my CV in application. Thank you very much for your time and consideration, and I look forward to hearing from you. Should you require any additional information, please contact me.
我的应征函中也附上了我的简历。谢谢您，期待您的回复。如果您需要任何其他信息，请与我联系。
I look forward to hearing from you. Should you require any additional information, please contact me.
期待您的回复。如果您需要任何其他信息，请与我联络。则显示出你对求职的主动与积极。

❷ 以 **Respectfully Yours、Yours Sincerely、Best Regards**（致敬）等词作为结束，再签名并且打上你的姓名。

英语履历表

要求应征者具备英语能力的公司，不管所要求的能力高低如何，都会要求应征者准备英语履历表，以下为英语履历表的范例：

Eric Lin
900-1 Dunhua East Rd.,
Taipei, 12032
Mobile phone number: 0900000000
Email: askme@gmail.com

Objective
Employment as engineer in an international* company

Work experience
2014-present Engineer, ABC Panel, Tainan, Taiwan

Responsibilities
Take charge of On-site machine operation and maintenance*
Prepare daily operation report
Provide support to factory operators

Education
2010-2014 Tainan University of Science and Technology
Bachelor of Science in Engineering

Additional Skills
Microsoft Office Suite
HTML programming
TOEIC 850
Proficient in spoken and written in English

Reference* available upon request

与求职信一样，履历表一开始必须列出**应征者的个人信息**，像姓名、通信地址、电子邮件地址和手机

开门见山说明 **Objective**（应征项目）
应征国际公司的工程师

按重要性排列，接着是 **Work experience**（工作经验）
2014 年迄今，台湾台南 ABC 面板公司工程师
注意 中文履历表通常都先列出时间比较久远的经历，而英语履历表则是先列出与目前时间较近的工作经历

Responsibilities（工作职责）则是说明你所负责的工作内容
负责现场机器的操作与维护
准备每日操作报告
支援厂房作业员

公司要求的**学历**部分在履历表中也必须列出
2010—2014 年台南科技大学工程科学学士

其他技能通常都是与电脑和语言相关的技能：
Microsoft Office 套装软体
HTML 程序
托业 850 分
英语听说流利

最后为了方便公司征询与表示诚意，会加上
Reference available upon request
（如有需求可以提供推荐人）

依据上面的英语范本，你只要把自己相关的信息套入，就可以产生一份属于你自己的英语求职信了。要记得求职信与简历表不能只提供完全一样的信息，而是应该在简历中好好强调个人的特色与优点。

实用句型

❶ I am very interested in this job position of _____.
我对 _____ 的工作职位非常有兴趣。

I am very interested in this job position of graphic designer.
我对平面设计师的工作职位非常有兴趣。

❷ I have more than _____ years of operation experiences in _____.
我在 _____ 有超过 _____ 年的经验。

I have more than five years of operation experiences in journalism.
我在新闻业有超过五年的经验。

❸ I major in _____.
我主修 _____。

主修科目举例
Political Science 政治学
Economics 经济学   Education 教育
Chemistry 化学   Accounting 会计

I major in literature.
我主修文学。

❹ I scored _____ in _____.
我在 _____ 得 _____ 分。

I scored 115 in TOEFL iBT.
我在托福测验中得 115 分。

单词补充　　♪ MP3 14-01

- **experience** [ɪkˈspɪrɪəns] n 经验
- **education** [ˌɛdʒuˈkeʃən] n 教育
- **qualification** [ˌkwɑləfəˈkeʃən] n 资格
- **professional** [prəˈfɛʃənl] a 职业的
- **Bachelor's Degree** n 大学学士学位
- **equivalent** [ɪˈkwɪvələnt] n 相同的 a 相等物
- **skill** [skɪl] n 技术
- **fundamental** [ˌfʌndəˈmɛntl] a 基础的
- **duty** [ˈdjutɪ] n 责任、职责
- **task** [tæsk] n 工作、任务
- **established** [əsˈtæblɪʃt] a 已建立的
- **supervision** [ˌsupɚˈvɪʒən] n 管理
- **assign** [əˈsaɪn] v 分配、指定
- **routine** [ruˈtin] n 例行公事 a 例行的
- **instruction** [ɪnˈstrʌkʃən] n 指示
- **candidate** [ˈkændədet] n 应征者
- **operation** [ˌɑpəˈreʃən] n 运作
- **industry** [ˈɪndəstrɪ] n 工业、行业
- **mechanics** [məˈkænɪks] n 机械学
- **high-tech** [ˈhaɪˈtɛk] a 高科技的
- **theoretical** [ˌθiəˈrɛtɪkl] a 理论的
- **equip** [ɪˈkwɪp] v 使有能力（资格）
- **philosophy** [fəˈlɑsəfɪ] n 哲学
- **enthusiasm** [ɪnˈθjuzɪˌæzəm] n 热忱
- **determination** [dɪˌtɝməˈneʃən] n 决心、坚定
- **consideration** [kənˌsɪdəˈreʃən] n 考虑
- **additional** [əˈdɪʃənl] a 附加的
- **international** [ˌɪntɚˈnæʃənl] a 国际的
- **maintenance** [ˈmentənəns] n 维持
- **reference** [ˈrɛfərəns] n 推荐、证明

Unit 2 英语面试

去面试之前，要先做好准备，所以先把基本的英语面试问题列出来吧！

Question 1 Please briefly introduce yourself. 请简单介绍你自己。

♪ MP3 14-02

I grew up in Taipei and attended National Taipei University of Science and Technology. My major was Tourism Management and I have been working at a travel agency for two years. I like singing and movies. I like challenges and I am good at getting along with * people. When I work, I always work very hard.

我来自台北，就读台北科技大学。我的主修是旅游管理，我在一家旅行社已经工作了两年。我喜欢唱歌及看电影。我喜欢挑战，擅长与人来往。我工作时都很认真。

▶ 这个问题的答案重点在于把你自己的背景跟优点介绍出来。注意下面句子的空格内容，这些是非常重要的基本信息，填入自己的信息后，在面试时大声说出来吧！

I grew up in _____ and attended _____ . My major was _____ and I have been working at _____ for _____ years. I like _____ and _____ . I like _____ .

我来自_____，就读_____。我的主修是_____，我在一家_____已经工作了_____年。我喜欢_____。

Question 2 Tell me about your strength and weakness.
请谈谈你的优缺点。

♪ MP3 14-03

For both of my strength * and weakness * , I would say that I am detail oriented. Since I always want to accomplish as much as possible, I pay my attention to details. For example, I pay a lot of attention to listen to customers. My attention to details helps me greatly in the field of work, but I also consider it as my weakness because I sometimes stress myself too much. I am learning how to get the balance between work and leisure.

我认为太过注重细节是我的优点及缺点。因为我总是想要多完成目标，我会把注意力放在细节上。例如，我很注意听取顾客意见。注重细节让我在工作上表现卓越。但是，我认为注重细节也是我的缺点，因为有时候我会给自己过多的压力。我正在学习如何在工作与休闲之间取得平衡。

▶ 这个问题如果只是一味地说明自己的优势，并没有办法在面试时争取到太多的印象分，反而坦诚谈谈自己的缺点才是上策，但是要记得把缺点包装成优势并且提出可能的解决方法。

154

Question 3 **Please give a specific example to show how you made things more efficient at your last job position.**

请举一个特定的例子说明在你自己的职位中如何让工作更有效率。

♪ MP3 14-04

As a ticketing clerk, I tried to figure out a more efficient processing way to handle ticketing by systematically arranging our work flow. It's something small, but my coworkers at the travel agency agreed and accepted my small invention of the simpler work flow that saves about five minutes per ticket we issue. Our manager came to me and appreciated* my help.

身为票务，我试着系统解决工作流程，找出更有效的处理票务方式。这只是小事，但是我旅行社的同事都同意并且接受我的更简易的工作流程小发明，我们现在每开一张票可以节约五分钟的时间。我们的经理还来向我致谢。

▶ 这个问题在回答时必须举例特定说明，也必须加上数字证据，像范例中的 "**that saves about five minutes for per ticket we issue**（我们现在每开一张票可以节约五分钟的时间）"，让你的回答更具说服力。

会话补充 Conversation ♪ MP3 14-05

A: Why should I hire you?
B: I have a strong determination. When I make up my mind, I'll try my best to finish the task.

A: 我为什么应该雇用你？
B: 我有很强的决心。当我下定决心时，会尽力完成工作。

单词补充 ♪ MP3 14-06

★ get along with
 ph 与……和睦相处
★ strength [strɛŋθ] n 优点
★ weakness [ˈwiknɪs] n 缺点
★ appreciate [əˈpriʃɪet] v 感激、欣赏

陈述已发生过的事情就要使用一般过去时，所以讲述你的工作经历时，要记得使用一般过去时。来看下面一则小故事，注意动词变化的地方！

Once upon a time, a poor farmer **lived** with his wife. One day, the farmer **dug up** his field and **found** a chest. He **took** the chest home and **showed** it to his wife. They then **kept** the chest home. One morning, his wife accidently **dropped** an apple into the chest. The farmer's wife **took** the apple out, but she **found** there were more apples in the chest no matter how many apples **were taken out**. The farmer and his wife then **sold** apples and **lived** a rich life.

从前有一位很穷的农夫跟他的妻子一起生活。有一天农夫在田里挖掘并且找到一个箱子。他把箱子带回家给妻子。之后，他们就把箱子放在家中。一天早上，他的妻子意外地把一颗苹果掉到箱子里。农夫的妻子把那颗苹果拿出来，但是她发现箱子中有更多的苹果，不管她拿出多少颗，箱子都一直还是有苹果。后来，农夫跟他的妻子就靠卖苹果为生，并且过着富裕的生活。

动词过去式变化的规则有：
❶ 规则变化：词尾 + **ed**；动词词尾有 e 者，直接加 **d**；动词字尾是 "辅音 + **y**" 者，去 **y** 加 **ied**；动词为 "辅音 + 元音 + 辅音" 排列，重复字尾加 **ed**
❷ 不规则变化：要个别记忆

> **语法教室**

学完了一般过去时，接下来我们要学习表示"假定、想象与愿望"的假设语气，我们分别来看与现在事实相反的假设语气、与过去事实相反的假设语气、与未来事实相反的假设语气。

假设语气的时态要比陈述事实的现在或过去一般时要来得早一点。以下面的句型为例：I wish + 与现在事实相反的希望

简单现在式

I have time to visit him. 我现在有时间去看他。
I wish I had time to visit him. 我希望我现在有时间去看他。

简单过去式

I had time to visit him last week. 我上星期有时间去看他。
I wish I had had time to visit him last week. 我希望我上星期有时间去看他。

❶ 与现在事实相反的假设语气

If + 主语 + 过去式动词 , 主语 + should / would / could / might + 原形动词

If you had time now, you might go to Japan for cherry blossom viewing. 如果你现在有时间，你就可以去日本看樱花。

❷ 与过去事实相反的假设语气

If + 主语 + 过去完成式动词 , 主语 + should / would / could / might + have + 过去分词

If you had had time last week, you might have gone to Japan for cherry blossom viewing. 如果你上周有时间，你那时就可以去日本看樱花。
If the strategic alliance between two sides had failed, there would have been no trust left.
如果双方的策略联盟失败了，信任就不存在了。

❸ 与未来事实相反的假设语气

If + 主语 + were to + 原形 , 主语 + should / would / could / might + 原形动词

If you were to have time, you should go to Japan for cherry blossom viewing. 如果你有时间，你应该去日本赏樱。（可能性比较低）
If the strategic alliance between two sides were to fail, there would be no trust left.
如果双方的策略联盟失败了，信任就不存在了。（可能性比较低）

Unit 3 用英语介绍自己

在工作中我们都有机会使用邮件或口头上介绍自己，现在就来学习如何在工作时向别人介绍自己。先来看看如何用电子邮件介绍自己。以下画线的句子是刚就职发电子邮件给他人时，常会用的句子，要学会。

Dear Mr. Williams,

My name is Eric Lin, and I have just been hired as the new Engineer here at DEF Panel to take charge of * machine operation and maintenance❶. Starting from March 31, I will be taking the role of James Chen❷. With this email, I would like to introduce myself and send my regards to you. You will also find my contact information in this email, and do contact me if you need any assistance *. I am very excited about joining the company, and I am looking forward to meeting you in person. I am always at your service.

All the best,

Eric Lin

Engineer, DEF Panel

威廉先生：
　　您好！我是艾瑞克·林，我是 DEF 面板公司新雇用的工程师，负责机器操作与维护。从 3 月 31 日起，我将接替詹姆斯·陈的工作。借此封电子邮件，我要向您介绍自己并且向您问候。在此封电子邮件中，您也可以获得我的联系信息，如果您需要任何协助，请联络我。我对于加入公司感到很振奋，也很期待与您会面。我会随时为您提供服务。

致敬

DEF 面板公司工程师
艾瑞克·林

实用句型

❶ I have just been hired as 职位 here at 公司 to take charge of _____.

我刚被 公司 雇用为 职位 负责 _____。

❷ Starting from 时间, I will be taking the role of 人名.

从 时间 开始，我将接替 人名 的工作。

157

接下来我们学习如何用英语向他人面对面地介绍自己,以到职第一天向同事们自我介绍为例。

Dear Colleagues,

I would like to introduce myself to you. I am Eric Lin, and I have been hired as an Engineering here at DEF Panel*. I will be working alongside all of you for machine operation and maintenance.

Before I joined DEF Panel, I worked in a similar* role at ABC Panel. I look forward to* working for the company and meeting my dear colleagues.

Today is my first day here, and I am very impressed of your devotion* to work. I am very passionate* about being part of your team. I know I will learn a lot from you, and I am very willing to contribute* to the success of the company.

I will be working at the shop floor most of the time, and my extension* is 3241. Do reach me whenever you need me. As people say, "The expert in anything was once a beginner." Please help me to become an expert like you. Thank you.

→ 第一天的自我介绍一样从称呼开始

→ 接着说明谈话用意、你的姓名、职称与负责的职务

→ 简单介绍自己之前的工作与对新公司与新同事的期待

→ 谈谈自己对新工作的第一天印象与自己的振奋、对自己的期待

→ 最后,提供可以联系你的信息,欢迎大家与你联系,使用引述寻求指导,结尾一定要谢谢各位同事

各位同事:
　　你们好,我想要跟大家介绍我自己。我是艾瑞克·林,是DEF面板新雇用的工程师。我将跟大家一起工作,负责机器操作与维护。
　　在加入DEF面板之前,我在ABC面板做类似的工作。我很期待在公司与各位一起合作。
　　今天是我第一天工作,我对于大家对于工作的投入印象深刻。能够加入这个团队我很振奋。我知道我将从各位身上学到非常多,我也很愿意为公司的成功做贡献。
　　我大部分的时间都会在,我的分机是3241。只要有需要,请联系我。就像人们说的:"任何专家都是从生手开始的。"请协助我,让我成为像各位一样的专家。谢谢你们!

单词补充 ♪ MP3 14-07
* **take charge of** ph. 负责
* **assistance** [əˈsɪstəns] n. 协助
* **panel** [ˈpænl] n. 面板
* **similar** [ˈsɪmələ] a. 相似的
* **look forward to** ph. 期待
* **devotion** [dɪˈvoʃən] n. 献身、忠诚
* **passionate** [ˈpæʃənɪt] a. 热情的
* **contribute** [kənˈtrɪbjut] v. 贡献
* **extension** [ɪkˈstɛnʃən] n. 电话分机

第一天上班是个令人紧张的经验,更何况要使用英语自我介绍,但是只要有诚意,同事们都可以感受得到,真的 **"The expert in anything was once a beginner."** 谁都有面对上班第一天的时候,用诚意与英语来介绍自己吧!

158

Unit 1  进行晨间会议

进入必须使用英语的工作环境后，有些职位势必得用英语进行说明、报告与提问，在 Lesson 15 里，我们跟着主角 Jay（杰）来看看一天中需要用英语进行的各个任务。以下是 Jay 在 2017 年 3 月 31 日要做的事情。

To Do List, March 31, 2016 (Thursday) 2017 年 3 月 31 日（星期四）应执行事项	
8:00—9:00	Morning Scheduling Meeting 每日排程会议
9:00—10:00	Office Work 办公室事务处理
10:00—12:00	Shop Floor Meeting 现场会议
12:00—13:00	Lunch Break 午餐休息时间
13:00—15:00	Visit of Wow Company Wow 公司来访
15:00—17:00	System Training 系统训练
17:00—18:00	Wrapping up for the Day 总结一天工作

语法教室

在职场上，成本是很重要的，不管是金钱上还是时间上的花费，都是上班族在做每项工作时需要考量的重要因素，在此学习用来表示"花钱""花时间"的 cost、pay、spend、take 的用法。

❶ 花钱

This pen costs me $100.（陈述事实）
= It costs me $100 to buy the pen.
I paid $100 for this pen.（过去的动作）
I spent $100 on this pen.（过去的动作）
= I spent $100 buying the pen. 这支笔花了我 100 美元。

❷ 花时间

It took me two weeks to finish the paper.
I spent two weeks on the paper.
I spent two weeks writing the paper.
Writing the paper took me two weeks.
我花了两周的时间写报告。

在使用时要特别注意以下几点：
1. 使用花钱与花时间的主语是人还是 it
2. 熟记动词与介词的搭配
3. 动词之后要接"不定词（to V）"还是"V-ing"

Lesson 15

在晨间会议上，会有不同的人进行报告，来听听经理的报告内容： ♪ MP3 15-01

Good morning, everyone.❶ Welcome to this morning's meeting. Michael will be absent from* this meeting.❶ We need to start the meeting now since we have a lot to be accomplished*.❷ Let's look at the agenda* on the slides*.❸

The first point is❹ we need to check and confirm* production orders scheduled*. We received an emergent* order released* from the sales department* yesterday afternoon. I need some clarification for the scheduling of the order in order to* let our people know whether we should start producing the order today or tomorrow.❺

Second, we need to come to a consensus* about the best solution* for the timely interruption* of emergent orders.❻ Because we need to deliver 2 million filters* daily for each machine, we now often have large emergent orders. I believe we need to spend❷ some time discussing the arrangement* of order sequence to figure out effective* strategies.❼

❶ 是报告人一开始就会招呼大家的用语
❷ 为了马上开始会议及提醒大家要有效率地开会，会议主持人会说的话
❸ 会议的议程都会打在投影仪上
❹ 开门见山地说：The first point / item is... 第一点 / 第一件事项为……
❺ 然后说明第一点或第一事项的背景
❻ 再说明第二点或第二件事项
❼ 再解释背景或原因

大家早，欢迎来参加今天的会议。麦克无法出席今天的会议。我们现在就开始开会，因为我们有很多事必须讨论。先来看看投影仪上的议程。

第一点是我们必须检查与确认已经排定的工单。昨天下午，我们收到销售部门开出的紧急订单。我需要厘清该订单的安排，以便让我们部门的人知道该订单应该今天或明天开始生产。

第二，我们必须达成共识，找出最佳的解决方法，决定紧急订单的即时插单。因为我们必须每日生产200万支滤嘴，我们现在常会有量较大的紧急订单。我认为我们必须花点时间讨论订单排序，以拟定有效策略。

实用单词   ♪ MP3 15-02

be absent from ph 缺席
accomplish [əˈkɑmplɪʃ] v 完成
agenda [əˈdʒɛndə] n 议程
slide [slaɪd] n 幻灯片
confirm v 确认
schedule [ˈskɛdʒul] v 排入计划
emergent [ɪˈmɝdʒənt] a 紧急的
release [rɪˈlis] v 释放、发表

sales department ph 销售部
in order to ph 为了
consensus [kənˈsɛnsəs] a 不断的
solution [səˈluʃən] n 解决方法
interruption [ˌɪntəˈrʌpʃən] n 打断、中止
filter [ˈfɪltɚ] n 滤器
arrangement [əˈrendʒmənt] n 安排
effective [ɪˈfɛktɪv] a 有效率的

可以依据工作中的实际晨会情况，从问候、议程及议题等听懂或进行开场简报。接下来看看 Jay 接手的任务安排简报：

🎵 MP3 15-03

❶ 开场
❷ 各部机器所排定的工单（从 ❷-1 到 ❷-4）
★ 任务安排的重要信息为：哪部机器何时生产多少数量的什么产品，使用什么原料或执行什么任务
❸ 宣布工作时间改变的注意事项
❹ 最后要让听取报告的人有机会提问

Next, I am going to report to you❸ the schedule* of today's production orders.❶ From Monday to Wednesday, Machine 001 is scheduled to produce* Order# AA at the amount* of 500,000 filters with Material BB.❷-1 On Thursday, Machine 001 will begin producing a different order with different material* at the amount of 300,000 filters.❷-2

Machine 002 and 003, at the same time, are both scheduled the whole week to produce Order #BB at the amount of 1 million filters respectively* by using Material DD.❷-3 For Machine 004, it is scheduled to run testing during noon time this week, and we would like to ask for the cooperation* of operators at the shop floor.❷-4 Your lunch schedule will be a little earlier this week, and do remember to shut down* the machine at 11:30 sharp for testing purposes*.❸ Please let me know if❹ you have any problems or concerns.❹

接着，我来报告今天的工单任务安排。从星期一到星期三，001 号机排定生产工单 # AA，生产数量为 500 000 支滤嘴，使用原料 BB。星期四时，机器 001 开始生产不同的工单，使用不同种类的原料，生产数量为 300 000 万支滤嘴。

机器 002 与 003 两部机器本周将同时排定生产工单 #BB，分别生产 100 万支滤嘴，使用原料 DD。机器 004 本周在中午时排定进行测试，我们需要现场作业人员的帮忙。这星期你们的午餐时间会提早些，并且基于测试目的，请记得在 11:30 分时准时停机。如果有任何问题与考量，请让我知道。

实用句型

❶ _____ will be absent from _____ .
_____ 无法出席 _____ 。

❷ I believe we need to spend _____ .
我认为我们必须花 _____ 。

❸ I am going to report to you _____ .
我来向你们报告 _____ 。

❹ Please let me know if _____ .
如果有 _____ ，请让我知道。

单词补充 🎵 MP3 15-04

★ schedule [ˈskɛdʒʊl] n 时程表
★ produce [prəˈdjus] v 生产
★ amount [əˈmaʊnt] n 数量
★ material [məˈtɪrɪəl] n 材料
★ respectively [rɪˈspɛktɪvlɪ] ad 分别地
★ cooperation [ko͵ɑpəˈreʃən] n 合作
★ shut down ph 关闭
★ purpose [ˈpɝpəs] n 目的

Unit 2 电子邮件往来

Jay 的下一个行程是要回办公室处理文书，他收到来自其他公司的询问电子邮件。

To:
Subject:

Dear Jay,

I'm John writing from Great Machine that provides* your company the machine system for production. I got your contact information* from your manager, Julian. He told me you are taking the role of Kevin and is in charge of machine system design. According to Julian, your company is now considering to have a new full automation* system to upgrade* the existing one. Would you please briefly* let us know what we can better assist you? We look forward to continuously* serving your company.

Yours Sincerely,

John Inoue
Director of System Design, Great Machine

杰：
　　您好，我是卓越机械的约翰，我们公司提供给你们公司生产用的机器系统。贵公司经理朱利安给了我您的联系信息。他告诉我您将接替凯文的职位，负责机器系统设计。根据朱利安所说的，贵公司正在考虑以全自动化系统来更新既有系统。您是否可以先简略地让我们知道要如何更进一步地服务您？我们期待持续服务贵公司。

致敬

约翰·上井
卓越机械系统设计部门主任

除了开头的介绍与说明邮件主旨和最后的礼貌性结语外，这封电子邮件中只有一个通盘性的问题 **Would you please briefly let us know what we can better assist you?**（您是否可以先简略地让我们知道要如何更进一步地服务您？）

接下来 Jay 针对对方提出的问题，简单地回了一封信。

To:
Subject:

Dear John,

    Thank you for your email. Yes, Julian instructed me about our current consideration of full automation. We are planning to replace the current 25% manual* operation. At present*, at each work station, two operators are taking care of three machines. We believe with the design of full automation, we are able to* allow two operators to be in charge of five machines. Robot arms will help us to do more work. That is the basic design concept we have now. Please give us feedback* about the feasibility*. Additionally*, we need quotation* and your proposed installation* time for the full automation. Once again, I would appreciate very much for your help.

Best Regards,

Jay
Engineer, System Design, ABC International

约翰：

    您好，谢谢您的邮件。是的，朱利安告知了我们目前的全自动化考量。我们计划取代目前 25% 的手动操作。目前，在每个工作站，两位作业员负责三台机器。我们相信借助全自动化设计，我们可以让两位作业员负责五台机器。机械手臂将可以帮助我们执行更多工作。这是我们目前的设计概念。请告知我们是否可行。此外，我们需要有全自动化的报价与您提议的安装时间。再次感谢您的协助。

致敬

杰
ABC 国际公司系统设计工程师

164

▶ 在这封回复对方的电子邮件中,我们看到以下几个重点:

先准备几句礼貌性用语:

- **Thank you for your email.**
  谢谢您的电子邮件。
- **Please give us feedback about the feasibility.**
  请告知我们是否可行。
- **Once again, I would appreciate very much for your help.**
  再次感谢您的协助。

使用收到的邮件内容作为开场回复:

- **Yes, Julian instructed me about our current consideration of full automation.**
  是的,朱利安告知了我们目前的全自动化考量。

之后再提供你要回复的信息:

- **We are planning to replace the current 25% manual operation.**
  我们计划取代目前 25% 的手动操作。
- **At present, at each work station, two operators are taking care of three machines. We believe with the design of full automation, we are able to allow two operators to be in charge of five machines.**
  我们相信借助全自动化设计,我们可以让两位作业员负责五部机器。
- **Robot arms will help us to do more work.**
  机械手臂将可以帮助我们执行更多工作。

　　先看懂对方的电子邮件,找出问题,再利用回复邮件中的前后礼貌性用语,加上各个情境中需要的信息,就可以适当地回复问题。

单词补充　♪ MP3 15-05

★ **provide** [prə'vaɪd] v 提供
★ **information** [ˌɪnfɚ'meʃən] n 信息
★ **automation** [ˌɔtə'meʃən] n 自动化操作
★ **upgrade** [ʌp'gred] n / v 升级
★ **briefly** ['brifli] ad 简短地
★ **continuously** [kən'tɪnjuəslɪ] ad 接连不断地
★ **manual** ['mænjuəl] a 手动的
★ **at present** ph 目前
★ **be able to** ph 能够
★ **feedback** ['fid,bæk] n 回馈
★ **feasibility** [ˌfizə'bɪlətɪ] n 可行性
★ **additionally** [ə'dɪʃənlɪ] ad 此外
★ **quotation** [kwo'teʃən] n 报价单
★ **installation** [ˌɪnstə'leʃən] n 安装

Unit 3 现场会议

依照今天须完成的工作行程，Jay 必须跟现场的人员开会，我们来看看他们的对话。

对话情境

♪ MP3 15-06

A : Hi, Jane. How are you doing today?
B : Hi, Jay. Fine, and how about you?
A : Busy but fine. How's the adjustment going this morning?
B : We have been trying to find the optimal setting for the drum well. We have seen some improvements, but we will work harder for better results.
A : Thank you very much. I believe we can have better results to reduce the air flow speed to the target range this afternoon, right?
B : Yes, that is our first priority.
A : Great, and this afternoon, we can then work on the maintenance of Machine 001.
B : Sure.

A: 嗨，珍。你今天好吗？
B: 嗨，杰。很好，你呢？
A: 很忙，但是很好。今天早上的调整进行得如何？
B: 我们一直试着找出鼓的最优化设定。我们有看到一些改善的情况，但是还是更努力地想有更好的结果。
A: 谢谢。我相信到了下午我们可以有更好的结果，可以减少气体流量速度，达到我们的目标范围，对吧？
B: 是的，那会是我们的首要目标。
A: 太好了，今天下午我们可以开始 001 机器的维修。
B: 当然。

　　现场会议因为工厂机器运作往往很嘈杂，所以不会像办公室会议一样，大家规规矩矩地坐下来开会，因此也较为快速与轻松些，但是重要的会议功能还是要顾及。

　　通常在简单的寒暄后，会马上询问：How's... going?（……进行如何？）之后再依据得到的答案，进一步询问或回应，例如：Thank you very much. I believe we can have better results to reduce the air flow speed to the target range this afternoon, right?（谢谢。我相信到了下午我们可以有更好的结果，可以减少气体流量速度，达到我们的目标范围，对吧？）

　　还要进一步把下午之后的预定工作项目提出来讨论：Great, and this afternoon, we can then work on the maintenance of Machine 001.（太好了，今天下午我们可以开始 001 机器的维修。）这样就可以很快地开完现场会议。

Unit 4 午休闲聊

对话情境　　　♪ MP3 15-07

A: Hi, Jay. Have you got a minute?
B: I am free to talk to you. What's going on?
A: I'm planning for a welcome party for you. Is this Friday night ok for you?
B: That sounds great. Thank you so much.

A：杰，你有空吗？
B：我有空，怎么了？
A：我正在策划你的欢迎派对。这个星期五你的时间可以吗？
B：太好了，谢谢你。

在职场上，不管是于公于私，都有安排活动的时候，所以一定要学好提出邀请、接受邀请、拒绝邀请的句子。邀请他人可用 **Do you want...?**（你想要……吗？）或 **Are you interested in...?**（你对……有兴趣吗？）

而如果要接受邀请，可以简单说 **OK!**（好！）或 **I'd love to.**（我愿意）或 **It's my honor.**（这是我的荣幸）

提出邀请　　♪ MP3 15-08

Do you want to join us for the basketball game after work?
下班后要加入我们的篮球赛吗？
Are you interested in the new Superman movie?
你想去看新的超人电影吗？
This weekend, our hiking club is going to Alishan, and will you join us?
这个周末，我们的踏青社要去阿里山，你愿意加入我们吗？

接受邀请　　♪ MP3 15-09

That sounds great! 太好了！
I am available, and I will be there.
我有空，我会去。
Thank you for inviting me, and I would be delighted.
谢谢邀请我，我很乐意去。

拒绝邀请　　♪ MP3 15-10

I am sorry; I have a meeting on Friday night.
抱歉，我星期五晚上有会议。
Thank you for the invitation, but I will have a family dinner to attend on that night.
谢谢邀请我，但是那天晚上我有家庭聚餐得出席。

Unit 5 公司参访

Jay 接下来的工作是接待来访的 Wow 公司工作人员，他必须向对方介绍公司与他的部门。

介绍公司

Jay 准备了 30 秒钟的 ABC 国际公司介绍如下： ♪ MP3 15-11

Distinguished guests of Wow Company, good day.❶
On behalf of ABC International, I would like to first welcome all of you to visit us. Let me briefly introduce ABC International to you.

ABC International is a member of ABC Tobacco* Group Companies. Established in 1990, ABC International is the third largest tobacco maker in Asia.❷ Today, we have all over 10,000 workers, and we operate in about 50 countries around the world.❸ We are proud to say that we are truly an international company with our employees from 60 countries.❹⁻¹ Furthermore, we set global environment, health, safety and sustainability * standards for our operations.❹⁻² Our company philosophy is striving for greatness.❺

❶ 开场属于万能句型，你可以把这些句子背下来，换成其他公司名称使用
❷ 介绍公司的背景
❸ 介绍公司员工与在全世界各地的营运
❹ 介绍公司的独特处（从 ❹-1 到 ❹-2）
❺ 提及公司的理念

Wow 公司的贵宾，大家好。
我谨代表 ABC 国际公司，首先欢迎各位莅临我们公司。让我简单为您介绍 ABC 国际公司。
ABC 国际公司隶属 ABC 香烟集团。成立于 1990 年，ABC 国际公司是全亚洲第三大香烟制造商。今天我们在全世界 50 多个国家市场雇用了 10 000 多位员工。我们很骄傲地告诉各位，我们是家真正的国际公司，我们的员工来自 60 个国家。再者，我们制定了全球环境、卫生与可持续性营运标准。本公司的理念是追求卓越。

实用句型

❶ 欢迎贵公司人员来访

Distinguished guests of ＿＿＿＿＿, good day.
＿＿＿＿＿ 公司的贵宾，大家好。

❷ 介绍公司的资历

Established in 年份, ＿＿＿＿＿ is ＿＿＿＿＿.
成立于 ＿＿＿＿＿ 年，＿＿＿＿＿ 是 ＿＿＿＿＿。

部门介绍

30 秒的公司介绍之后，Jay 要介绍他的工作部门 system design（系统设计）。

🎵 MP3 15-12

I now introduce you my department, System Design. The function of System Design Department is to❶ define the architecture *, components *, modules *, interfaces * and data for a system to satisfy the requirements * of production. As you can see on the slide, we need to decide various parameters when design the system. We also need to follow global standards * set by our head office. The quotation from the well-known social entrepreneur, John Wood, that "It's the little details that are vital; little things make big things happen" can best describe our work at the Department of System Design.❷ With that, I would like to finish my introduction to you today. My co-worker, Tony, will be taking over and will be your guide to continue your company tour.❸ Any or all questions are welcome. Thank you.

现在我来向大家介绍我的部门，系统设计部门。系统设计部门的任务是定义系统的结构、组成、模块、界面与资料，让系统能够符合生产需求。如大家在投影仪上看到的，在设计系统时，我们必须遵照总公司拟定的全球标准。知名社会企业家约翰伍德的话最能够说明我们系统设计部的工作，"细节才是重点，小事才能成就大事。"这就是我今天的介绍。我的同事托尼接下来将会带大家继续您今天的参访。欢迎您提问。谢谢。

语法教室

❶ When she finished her piano practice, she felt tired.

　　= Finishing her piano practice, she felt tired.
　　练习完钢琴后，她觉得很累。

❷ When she was caught, she was talking to me.

　　= Being caught, she was talking to me.
　　被捕时，她在跟我说话。

❸ As he is a fan of Chien-Ming Wang, he is thrilled for the news that Wang would return to the majors.

　　= Being a fan of Chien-Ming Wang, he is thrilled for the news that Wang would return to the majors.
　　因为是王建民的粉丝，王建民即将返回大联盟的消息让他感到很兴奋。

实用句型

单词补充 MP3 15-13

★ **tobacco** [tə'bæko] n 烟草
★ **sustainability** [sə,stenə'bɪlətɪ] n 持续性、可持续性
★ **architecture** ['ɑrkətɛktʃɚ] n 结构；建筑
★ **component** [kəm'ponənt] n 零件
★ **module** ['mɑdʒul] n 模块
★ **interface** ['ɪntɚfes] n 界面
★ **requirement** [rɪ'kwaɪrmənt] n 需要
★ **standard** ['stændɚd] n 标准

❶ The function of _____ Department is to _____ .
_____ 部门的任务是 _____ 。

❷ The quotation from _____ can best describe our work _____ .
_____ 的引言最能描述我们 _____ 的工作。

❸ _____ will be take over and be your guide to _____ .
_____ 接下来将会带大家进行 _____ 。

对话情境

♪ MP3 15-14

A: Welcome to ABC company. I am Jay, your guide for today's company tour.

B: Nice to meet you, Jay. Patty Smith here.

A: The pleasure is mine. According to our email communication, the purpose of today's visit is to get to know about our operations.

B: That's correct. Thank you for your assistance.

A: Miss Smith, following our production process, we will start from the production area.

B: Surely.

A: We request you to put on a safety helmet and use ear plugs.

B: I understand safety always comes first.

A：欢迎来到 ABC 公司，我是杰，您今天来访的接待。

B：很高兴见到您，杰。我是帕蒂·史密斯。

A：我的荣幸。依据我们的电子邮件往来，您今天来访的目的是要了解我们的营运。

B：没错。谢谢您的协助。

A：史密斯小姐，依照制造流程，我们会从制造区域开始。

B：好的。

A：我们规定您要戴上安全帽，并且使用耳塞。

B：我了解安全第一。

Unit 6 进行训练

Jay 接下来的工作是要提供系统训练给操作人员。 ♪ MP3 15-15

Welcome to join our training this afternoon.❶ This system training is provided for new employees like you.❶❷ I will guide* you on how to operate the system step by step*. You will have plenty of* time to learn from me. I will also give you time for hands-on* operation.❸ Because this system is critical* for the operation on the shop floor, you need to pay attention to all details.❹ You are welcome to interrupt* me if you are not clear* about anything I say.❺ Meanwhile, I would also like to❷ ask your cooperation by switching your cell phones off*.❻ I believe now we can start❸ our training, and we will have a happy time to learn together this afternoon.❼

❶ 欢迎信息
❷ 说明系统训练对象
❸ 告知训练程序，让参加训练的人员安心
❹ 告知训练的重要性
❺ 鼓励提问
❻ 请大家合作
❼ 以鼓励大家作为结尾

　　欢迎来参加我们下午的训练。这节训练课程是提供给各位新员工的。我会一步一步地带着大家学习系统操作。各位会有足够的时间来学习。我也会给大家实际操作的时间。因为这个系统对现场的作业很关键，大家必须注意所有细节。如果各位有问题，可以随时打断我。同时，我也要请大家与我合作，请将您的手机关闭。我想我们现在可以开始训练了，今天下午我们会一起快乐地学习。

实用句型

❶ This _____ is provided for _____ like you.
这 _____ 是提供给你们 _____。

❷ Meanwhile, I would also like to _____.
同时，我也想要 _____。

❸ I believe now we can start _____.
我相信我们现在可以开始 _____。

单词补充 ♪ MP3 15-16

* guide [gaɪd] n./v. 带领、指导
* step by step ph. 步骤
* plenty of ph. 许多
* hands-on ['hændz'ɑn] a. 亲自动手的
* critical ['krɪtɪkl] a. 关键的
* interrupt [ˌɪntəˈrʌpt] v. 打断
* clear [klɪr] a. 清楚的
* switch off ph. 关闭（电器）

因为信号在系统操作时特别重要，所以 **Jay** 特别说明关于信号警示的内容。跟着 **Jay** 的工作行程，学完了一天中在工作场合中会用到的英语，接下来可以整理与复习一下，好好地依据实际的工作情况来使用。

♪ MP3 15-17

LED warning lights* on equipment* provide operators* on the shop floor with visual* and audible* indicators* to get to know the state* of a machine. In our system, there are red, yellow and green warning lights, and their functions are: red showing machine failures* such as emergent stop; yellow, over temperature* or pressure conditions; and green, normal* operation. For the smooth* operation of our production line*, each of you needs to closely* monitor* the colors of the LED warning lights.

设备上的 LED 警示灯给现场操作人员视觉与听觉警示，来了解机器的状态。在我们的系统中，有红、黄与绿色警示灯，它们的功能分别为：红色显示机器故障，如紧急停机；黄色显示温度或压力过高；绿色显示正常运作。为了让我们的生产线操作顺利，在座的每一位必须仔细观察 LED 警示灯的颜色。

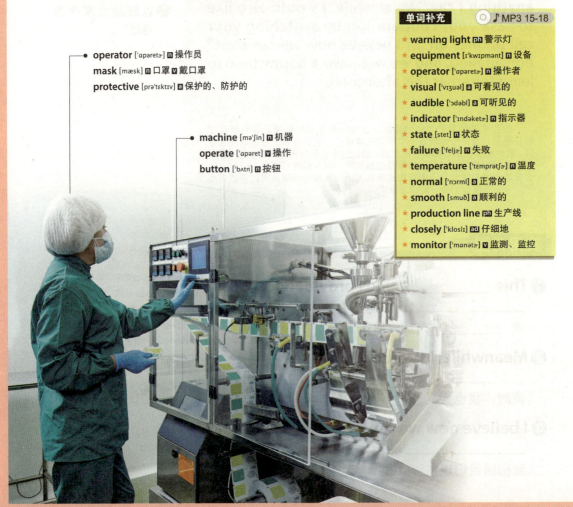

operator [ˈɑpəretɚ] n 操作员
mask [mæsk] n 口罩 v 戴口罩
protective [prəˈtɛktɪv] a 保护的、防护的

machine [məˈʃin] n 机器
operate [ˈɑpəret] v 操作
button [ˈbʌtn] n 按钮

单词补充 ♪ MP3 15-18

★ warning light n 警示灯
★ equipment [ɪˈkwɪpmənt] n 设备
★ operator [ˈɑpəretɚ] n 操作者
★ visual [ˈvɪʒuəl] a 可看见的
★ audible [ˈɔdəbl] a 可听见的
★ indicator [ˈɪndəketɚ] n 指示器
★ state [stet] n 状态
★ failure [ˈfeljɚ] n 失败
★ temperature [ˈtɛmprətʃɚ] n 温度
★ normal [ˈnɔrml] a 正常的
★ smooth [smuð] a 顺利的
★ production line n 生产线
★ closely [ˈkloslɪ] ad 仔细地
★ monitor [ˈmɑnətɚ] v 监测、监控

版权专有　侵权必究

图书在版编目（CIP）数据

翻转人生的15堂英语课／吴宜铮著．—北京：北京理工大学出版社，2019.7
ISBN 978-7-5682-7228-5

Ⅰ.①翻…　Ⅱ.①吴…　Ⅲ.①英语—自学参考资料　Ⅳ.①H31

中国版本图书馆CIP数据核字（2019）第135013号

北京市版权局著作权合同登记号图字：01-2017-2401
简体中文版由我识出版社有限公司授权出版发行
翻转人生的15堂英语课：英文能力由负转正，人生就此逆转胜！，吴宜铮
著，2016年，初版
ISBN：9789869267847

出版发行／北京理工大学出版社有限责任公司
社　　址／北京市海淀区中关村南大街5号
邮　　编／100081
电　　话／（010）68914775（总编室）
　　　　　（010）82562903（教材售后服务热线）
　　　　　（010）68948351（其他图书服务热线）
网　　址／http://www.bitpress.com.cn
经　　销／全国各地新华书店
印　　刷／北京紫瑞利印刷有限公司
开　　本／787毫米×1092毫米　1/16
印　　张／11.5　　　　　　　　　　　　　　　责任编辑／王俊洁
字　　数／305千字　　　　　　　　　　　　　　文案编辑／王俊洁
版　　次／2019年7月第1版　2019年7月第1次印刷　责任校对／周瑞红
定　　价／58.00元　　　　　　　　　　　　　　责任印制／李志强

图书出现印装质量问题，请拨打售后服务热线，本社负责调换